CHRISTIAN
FUNERALS

Andy Langford

Abingdon Press
NASHVILLE

CHRISTIAN FUNERALS

Copyright © 2010 by Abingdon Press

All rights reserved.

This book is printed on acid-free paper.

Library of Congress Cataloging-in-Publication Data

Langford, Andy.
    Christian funerals / Andy Langford.
        p.   cm.
    ISBN 978-1-4267-1138-1 (book—pbk./trade pbk. : alk. paper)   1. Funeral service.   I. Title.
    BV199.F8L36 2010
    265'.85—dc22

                                                                2010044848

Scripture quotations unless noted otherwise are taken from the New Revised Standard Version of the Bible, copyright 1989, Division of Christian Education of the National Council of the Churches of Christ in the United States of America. Used by permission. All rights reserved.

Scripture quotations marked (KJV) are taken from the King James or Authorized Version of the Bible.

Copyright page continued on pages 143-144.

10 11 12 13 14 15 16 17 18 19—10 9 8 7 6 5 4 3 2 1

MANUFACTURED IN THE UNITED STATES OF AMERICA

CONTENTS

PREFACE

Christian worship in the midst of death is the liturgical, formal, poetic, communal, and biblical expression of personal and community loss and grief as well as comfort and hope through the resurrection of Jesus Christ. This book is the indispensable resource for pastors caring for the dying, the dead, and the bereaved. This collection of the highest quality funeral resources, along with practical advice across a wide spectrum of Christian traditions, allows pastors to choose among many prayers, Scripture lessons, and liturgies. The resources come primarily from authorized denominational books of worship. Full Scripture texts are also included. Many pastors will carry a copy of this book with them every time they visit homes, hospitals, and hospice houses, and as they lead funerals, memorial services, and graveside committals.

CHAPTER ONE

MINISTRY AND WORSHIP AT TIMES OF DEATH

A Theological Consideration of Death

In 1997, thirty-three million persons in the United States watched on television the funeral of Lady Diana, Princess of Wales. From historic Westminster Abbey, two-and-a-half billion people around the world watched the solemn procession, heard sacred music, listened to her brother's eulogy, enjoyed Elton John singing "Candle in the Wind," and most significantly, heard the reading of Scripture and classic Anglican prayers. More people, through the power of the media, may have participated in this service of Christian worship than any other event in the twentieth century.

In 2009, thirty-one million persons in the US watched the television spectacular of Michael Jackson's memorial service. In this show, speakers occasionally mentioned God and many artists performed. Was it worship?

When powerful politicians, significant leaders of commerce, and renowned persons die, funerals and memorial services remain critical moments in the life of individuals and communities. How do Christians celebrate these moments in ways that honor the deceased and worship our God?

Just as important, however, are the smaller, quieter moments in homes, hospitals, sanctuaries, funeral homes, columbariums, and graveyards in every community. The prayers for a child not surviving birth, a memorial for a youth who died too young, the service for a beloved mother or father, and the committal of an older person with no family are just as significant and demand the same honor as those for any other person created in the image of God. Christianity proclaims that each individual is a unique child of God, no matter how famous or infamous, the age of the person, or the circumstance of his or her death. When anyone dies, at those moments the church offers God's blessing. Acts of Christian worship in the midst of death are the liturgical, formal, poetic, communal, and biblical expressions of personal and community loss and grief as well as comfort and hope through the resurrection of Jesus Christ.

People of all cultures and faiths honor persons at their death. Evidence of funeral practices goes back 300,000 years, even before the time of modern *Homo sapiens*. Today, some persons and families prefer to ignore death, or treat it as a simple passage from life, or create temporary collections of flowers and stuffed animals. In every place and time, persons gather to give thanks for the person who has died, comfort the families who grieve, and give reassurance to one another.

Christians, however, mark death with unique rituals that stand at the heart of our faith. Christians at all times and in all places acknowledge the reality of death and proclaim the promise of resurrection. Gathering in the power of the resurrected Jesus Christ, pastors guide a community's worship with the right Scriptures and with the appropriate prayers in a sacred space.

The heart of our Christian faith proclaims life beyond death. Jesus Christ in the Great Three Days from Holy Thursday to the Day of Easter died and lived again for our salvation and all of creation. Whenever the followers of Jesus Christ gather, from daily prayers to weekly worship to Easter festivals, we proclaim the mystery of death and resurrection

2

with joy and thanksgiving. In our prayers and worship, we accept the reality of death, remember the deceased, and honor those who have departed. In addition, we enable the family and believing community to witness to our shared faith. Together, persons share pain and joy, support one another, pray as one, and exhibit grief. Ultimately, we reaffirm God's covenant with us, with the saints, and with each other. For Christ's followers, salvation is first and foremost Christ's gift of life beyond death. Funerals and memorial services, along with all the services related to them, are the foundation stone of the ministry of the church.

Various ministries with the dying, a Christian funeral or memorial service, and then care for the grieving all mark significant passages in the Christian community. Faced with the reality of death, the people of God gather together to proclaim the good news: Jesus Christ has triumphed over death. Acknowledging grief and loss, the community remembers the person who has passed from the church on earth—"the church militant"—to the church in heaven—"the church triumphant." And in proclaiming the faith and acknowledging grief, God through the church grants comfort, hope, and resurrection to the whole body of Christ.

The Role of the Pastor

Pastors are the people ultimately responsible to ensure that every ministry and service for every person is the best possible expression of our Christian faith. The Christian pastor's role at death includes a wide range of ministries: from counseling and praying with the dying, being present at the time of death, planning and leading services of worship, caring for the grieving, and remembering the dead and their families long after funerals and memorial services. In every case, pastors offer comfort to the dying, hope to the bereaved, and a clear Christian witness to the whole community.

Unfortunately, on many occasions death occurs without advance notice. Every pastor has received an unexpected phone call in the middle of the night, or while on vacation, or in the midst of many other obligations. Death always shifts a pastor's life and a congregation's rhythm and reminds us of the central truth of Christianity: that death does not separate us from the love of God.

Ministries at times of death present many emotional and intellectual challenges for pastors. Even in their grief, families, pastors, and other helping professionals make many decisions quickly, such as the date and time for a service of worship. Often, services must be put together with little previous preparation. Pastors and families must decide in a few hours which Scriptures to read, who will participate, which songs to sing, and many other decisions, which may even change in the last moments. For at least a few days, and sometimes for many days or even months, ministering to the dying, the dead, and their loved ones becomes the single most important ministry of the people of God and their pastors.

Pastors experience no greater honor in ministry than standing at the bed of a dying person or presiding at funerals and memorial services. In my own pastoral ministry, I have presided at services for a stillborn child, a sixteen-year-old youth who suffered a heart attack, a youth with prolonged cancer, a suicide victim, the victim of a crime, a father of young children, members of my own family including my grandmothers and father, and hundreds of older adults. In every case, the words, distinctive music, signs, and silence during these days conveyed the love of God to family and a whole congregation. Standing beside a casket, speaking to people whom one cares for deeply, and proclaiming the Gospel of Resurrection is one of the highest privileges of ministry.

On these occasions, the pastor gathers the collective memory of the family and offers God's witness to those who mourn. Ministry at the time of death at its best faces death realistically, offers God's comfort, allows grief to be expressed, and honors the deceased as a unique creation of God. Pastors offer the liturgical, theological, and pastoral guidance that enhances the spiritual growth of everyone.

Pastors know, of course, that such ministry does not begin only at a time of death. Pastors must address issues of mortality and immortality within a congregation or among the people with whom one serves throughout one's ministry. Pastors have the responsibility to teach and preach about death, dying, and resurrection. Preach a sermon series and teach a class concerning death and dying. Create a planning guide for funerals. Invite a funeral director to teach about preplanning or simply answer questions. Arrange a tour of a funeral home. Host a member of a local hospice to speak. Offer classes to encourage persons to make end-of-life plans. Ask a lawyer to speak about wills and designating memorials. Lead a Bible study on biblical views of death. Plan carefully for special services such as All Saints Day, Homecoming, cemetery Decoration Day, and other special occasions when death and resurrection are the core theme. Encourage persons under hospice care or others clearly facing their own death to begin planning for their final days and their own funeral. These are essential ministries, however, which are not covered in this resource.

The resources in this book are a collection of the best Christian resources available to assist pastors specifically in their ministries of worship with persons at the time of death. This collection of the highest quality funeral resources, along with practical advice across a wide spectrum of Christian traditions, allows pastors to choose easily among many prayers, Scripture lessons, and liturgies. The resources come primarily from authorized denominational books of worship. Full Scripture texts are also included. Pastors do not need to juggle Bibles and prayer books and other collections of resources. All the resources pastors need at a time of death are here!

When a person is dying, family and friends gather around the terminally ill person. Medical professionals, such as hospice physicians and staff, stand alongside the family. See the Ministry with the Dying on page 13 for pastoral prayers and acts of worship with persons and families in times when death is on the near horizon.

Between the time of death and the time of the funeral or memorial service, a variety of supportive ministries by church, family, friends, and other organizations may take place. See A Family Hour, Wake, or Vigil on page 36 for guidance and direction.

When death has occurred, pastors and families must consider many topics regarding Services of Death and Resurrection. Traditionally, a "Funeral" is a service at death with the body or remains of the deceased present. A "Memorial Service" is a service without the remains of the deceased. "Burial of the Dead" is appropriate for a service at the location where the remains of the deceased are buried. The majority of this book provides resources for such Services of Death and Resurrection.

General Practical Guidelines

Before looking at all the specific acts of worship included in this book, let us focus first on some preliminary issues about funerals and memorial services in particular. At almost all Services of Death and Resurrection, many of the same questions arise every time.

Who should plan the final service? Common courtesy and practical wisdom dictates that the pastor and the bereaved family plan together the final service of worship, including many of the following subjects. Families often appreciate when pastors offer them options. For example, instead of just asking for favorite Scriptures or hymns, in which case most families simply say what seems most familiar, a pastor may provide a family with a list of possible Scriptures and hymns. In summary, neither the family nor the pastor should plan the service alone.

In addition, at the time of a loved one's death, funeral directors and other service providers are invaluable colleagues when planning the final service. While sometimes the subject of some negative stereotypes, the vast majority of these professionals are there to serve in any way possible. A good working relationship between pastors and funeral directors serves the dying and their families well.

Making decision, however, can cause stress. Especially at times of death, many families agonize too much over making "perfect" decisions, often with little time to decide. One role for the pastor is to reassure each family that whatever decisions are reached together, the family's plans will be honored and not critiqued at a later date.

When will the service occur? This is often the first decision, and the best time is the one that best meets the desires and schedules of family, friends, congregation, pastor, and funeral home. Ask if there are scheduling conflicts with the church, cemetery, or funeral home. Services may be held morning, afternoon, or night. Some services are preceded or followed by family gatherings, receptions of friends, committals, and meals. Some services occur immediately, and others may take weeks to arrange. Ultimately, the ideal time is simply the time set after conversations with everyone.

Where will the service take place? The place of worship shapes the service in many ways. Ideally, a sanctuary where the deceased worshiped should be used. In this sacred space, the person may have marked passages of Christian life such as baptism and marriage. The cost of a service in the sanctuary may also be lower. Ready access to the symbols of faith, hymns, and musical instruments are all valuable.

If the service is at the church, members of the staff or volunteers need to be alerted to set up the sanctuary or worship space. The placement of flowers, candles, paraments, banners, and other signs is crucial. When will the doors of the church be opened? Is the air conditioning or heat on? Who will usher?

A funeral chapel or home is also appropriate for the service. For the convenience of the family, sometimes the location and space of the funeral home works best. A family home, mausoleum, crematorium, columbarium, or even in the out-of-doors on land or sea are often also acceptable places for funerals and memorial services.

Graveside services are becoming more popular. This simple setting when the departed will be committed to the earth adds to the reality of death. The loss, however, of sacred space and symbols limits some options. Weather is also a concern, and bad weather will shorten the service.

Will the body be buried or cremated? In human history, the norm has been burial of a body in the ground where the body gradually returns to the earth. Burial of a body in a grave or tomb was historically the appropriate way to honor the dead. The gravesite may then be marked for generations to come. In a "Green Funeral" the body is buried without being embalmed or other ways to protect the body from the elements. The Jewish community requires burial, and some Christian communions, such as Roman Catholics and the Orthodox, have a strong preference for burial as a sign of respect for the dead. Yet embalming a body and placing it in a watertight casket seems to defeat the vision of returning the deceased to the earth. The cost is also higher.

Is cremation acceptable? The word *cremation* comes from the Latin that means "to burn" and specifically the burning of the dead. Typically, cremation involves burning the body for about four hours. The remains, called "cremains," appear as a white, chalky, and gritty powder from the bones. Does cremation have biblical warrant? In ancient Israel, the only bodies burned were those of idols, criminals, and enemies. In the New Testament, hell is described as a place of deep burning. Yet, cremation is more economical and allows the cremains to be scattered in various places. The dust of the remains can just as honorably be returned to the earth (either by gently sprinkling the ashes in a beloved setting or burying them in a small hole in an urn) or scattered on a body of water. If God can resurrect a body, God can also resurrect cremains. Most Christian communions now allow cremation, sometimes with qualifications, and the practice is clearly becoming more popular.

Many other questions need to be answered by the pastor and others planning the service. Will there be a worship bulletin? What will it include? Who will design it, print it, and fold it? See page 41 for a sample bulletin outline.

When the service is at the church or sanctuary, what colors are appropriate for the Communion table or altar, the pulpit, and other sanctuary fabrics? While some ancient traditions dictate black or white, today many congregations use many different colors including white and green as signs of life beyond death.

What will the pastor wear? This decision depends almost entirely on one's religious tradition. Most pastors wear what they wear on Sunday mornings: from a suit to robes to albs to chasubles (especially when the Eucharist is celebrated). Stoles worn with robes and albs may be white or green to any stoles used for either Lent or Easter.

What symbols and signs are appropriate? A paschal candle, a large white candle, may serve as a sign of the light in the midst of the darkness of death. A family Bible, a picture of the deceased, or a valued object or family mementos may be set in the worship space. One family encouraged persons to bring signs that remembered the deceased. In response, persons brought a small college mascot, a deck of playing cards, family pictures, and cherished earrings, among other signs. In no case, however, should such items hide or distract from the primary objects and signs in the sanctuary.

What about the coffin, casket, or urn? A coffin or urn with the cremains (the ashes after cremation) reminds persons of the reality of death. Typically, the coffin remains closed throughout the final service. Traditionally, the head of the coffin is away from the altar/table, except in the case of clergy, when the head is toward the altar/table. Many congregations make the decision primarily on the basis of tradition and architecture.

May the service be open to family and invited guests alone? A closed service sometimes is the appropriate decision. When a child has died in childbirth, a person has died in prison or under suspicious circumstances, the grief of family members is too great, or the family of a public figure needs some quiet space, it may be best to limit attendance at the funeral to just close family and friends. Closed services, however, are the exception.

Who participates? Ideally, the deceased's pastor leads the service. If the family determines that other pastors or persons are also to participate, pastoral courtesy suggests that the host pastor call and invite other participants and assign their roles. If a pastor is invited to participate in a service not in one's own congregation, good pastoral ethics dictate that one defer all decisions to the host pastor. A guest pastor should not try to come in and take over the service but understand his or her role as supportive and secondary.

Members of the deceased's family, friends, and members of the congregation may also participate in the service. Family and friends may read Scripture, sing songs, lead prayer, read an obituary, and give thanks for the life of the deceased. Inviting persons in advance adds to the quality of the service. See the section on Naming and Witness on page 104 for more information about how to involve laity in the service.

Another way to involve family and friends is the tradition of pallbearers to accompany or carry the casket. Pallbearers may need to be able to carry a casket, or simply serve as honorary persons to accompany an urn. Family members, friends, representatives of civic or military groups may all serve as pallbearers. Remember that women as well as men may serve as pallbearers.

What about the music? Who will play the piano, organ, flute, harp, guitar, or other instruments? Church musicians often have wisdom and experience to help the family and pastor with music. Congregational hymns are the simplest way to involve the whole congregation in worship. Solos, small choral groups, and choirs may also add to the liturgy. Musicians in particular need the earliest possible notification about worship.

How will the family participate? The family, who enter immediately before the beginning of a funeral or memorial service, typically sit together at the front of the congregation. The family may best work through their grief by singing hymns, joining in prayer, and speaking during the service. One family had all the grandchildren recite a poem together in honor of their deceased grandfather.

Should children participate in the activities around a death? Children, depending on their age and sensitivity, should be invited to be present at all these services. Hiding children from death ultimately does not serve them well. Allowing children to participate in the activities around a death may actually cause them less stress and fear. Their imaginations often conjure up a far worse picture than what is actually occurring.

How will the congregation participate? The community, through prayer, hymns, naming, witnessing, creeds, and Holy Communion confront death, comfort one another, and offer hope of new life. Often the congregation's greatest support is simply its physical presence, surrounding the family with familiar faces.

What about flowers and other signs of respect? Flowers can be signs of honor and respect for both the deceased and family. Yet, too many flowers may overwhelm the family and be a wasteful expense. The family may wish to limit the flowers to ones they alone purchase, for example as a spray on a casket. Florists must be careful never to cover up the symbols of the church such as the Communion table or altar, baptismal font, or cross. Simplicity and appropriateness are the guiding principles.

A pall or flag? A pall is a large cloth, often with an elaborate border or appliqué, which completely covers a casket. The pall serves as a sign of oneness in Christ by all believers. A national flag may be used as a sign of military service to one's country or simply one's love of the nation. Either may be placed on the casket by family members or others. In either case, flowers should not be put on the pall or flag. Before the burial, the flag should be folded and presented to the family.

Fraternal, civic, or military rites? Fraternal order and military and civic honors often occur as a last rite before burial or interment. For example, civic groups, military personnel, firefighters, police, and others have their own traditions at the death of a colleague. For Christian services, pastors should ensure that non-Christian rituals are secondary to the central proclamation of the gospel. Some churches allow such order and honors only before a service begins or immediately before the committal. This pattern preserves the integrity of the Christian service and allows the last words to be words of God's grace. Yet, certain acts— such as giving the flag, playing rifle volleys, and performing the music "Taps"—may best follow the committal. Decide early if there will be such rites and when they will occur.

Masonic final rites are distinctive. While not a religion, the Masonic organization believes in God. Some denominations allow a Mason ritual at the committal, but other traditions do not. Typically, a number of Masons, who consider one another brothers even if they have never met, may attend the service as a sign of respect and affection. The Masons will wear white gloves and lambskin aprons. If invited, they share a few signs including an evergreen branch (the Sprig of Acacia) as a symbol of eternal life and the white leather apron as a sign of their fraternity. The service is recited by one man from memory and may take from ten to twenty minutes. They conclude their ritual with a prayer and words of comfort for the family.

Military final rites are also distinctive. Allowed only for eligible veterans at the request of a family, at least two persons represent the military at the service as an honor guard at no expense to the family. The ritual may include rifle shots. The service always includes the folding of the flag of the United States of America and a presentation of the flag to the family on behalf of a grateful nation. The folding of the flag into a triangle is a reminder of the hats worn by some of America's earliest soldiers and sailors. The service also always concludes with a bugler (or electronic bugle) playing "Taps." "Taps," a nineteenth century song, became a part of all military funerals in 1891. The melancholy yet peaceful notes sounding the end of the day are poignant and powerful. Rarely do words need to be said at the end of "Taps."

With all these decisions reached, it is now time for the pastor to plan the specific ministries of the church.

All of the resources within this book can be used in any kind of ministry and service. The Scriptures throughout this resource come primarily from the New Revised Standard Version of the Holy Bible. In a few cases, other translations have been used, such as the King James Version of Psalm 23. In a number of cases, the text has been slightly changed (the sign "alt." will appear) to make the text clearer for the public reading of Scripture. Primarily, these involve changing indefinite pronouns—he, she, and it—to proper names, such as "Jesus," for clarity in oral communication. Most of the texts appear in "sense lines" that assist in reading the texts in public with appropriate breaks. On occasion, in a longer text, "[ ]" denotes verses that may not be included.

One way to use this book is to mark each act of worship to be used. For example, the pastor may simply mark each act of worship with a small tag or sticky note, starting at the top of the first page with the first act of worship and going down to the bottom of the last page with the act of worship. As the service proceeds, simply turn to the next tag.

May God bless all pastors in their ministry in the midst of death as they bear witness to the reality of death and promise of resurrection!

CHAPTER TWO

MINISTRY WITH THE DYING

When death is near, pastors are often summoned to a home, hospital, or hospice. The pastor represents the living Body of Christ in such times of crisis, and the words and actions make Jesus Christ present to everyone. This ministry with the dying extends to the person dying, gathered family, and persons who support the patient and the family. This ministry also includes the medical and other professionals, who are often present during a pastor's visit, who support the dying and the family in many ways.

The following resources provide a range of words and actions that communicate the living presence of Jesus Christ before death and possibly at the very moment of death. The ancient and sacramental title for these collective acts in the Roman Catholic tradition is "extreme unction" or "last rites."

Simply being present with a quiet voice, a warm hug, and the appropriate words provides strength and comfort to everyone. This is not the time for idle conversation or inappropriate levity. Ask oneself the old question, "How would Christ act in this situation?" The pastor is the embodiment of the body of Christ in these moments. Some pastors wear a simple stole over their clothing during these times to signify the holy moment.

These times may be moments of significant healing and growth for everyone involved. The dying may speak words or give signs of forgiveness or ask for forgiveness. The gathered family may be reunited not only with the dying person but also with one another. At death, pretenses may be let down and true reconciliation take place. Family may encourage the dying to let go of life, and family may be helped in letting go. Encourage such holy conversation.

Ministry with the dying may also be a time to begin preparing for a funeral or memorial service. Especially in the last days, the pastor may encourage both the person dying and the family to begin thinking about the many decisions that need to be made. Funerals and memorial services are significantly better when everyone knows that decisions were made with the assistance of the departed.

Sometimes, families refuse to consider such issues, one manifestation of a denial of death. With gentle pastoral encouragement, however, the pastor may assist in helping persons move through the stages of grief. Often, in the midst of grief, dealing with such decisions both brings to reality the immediacy of death and helps one look toward the future. Who will write the obituary? What should this remembrance include? Has pre-planning been done with the funeral home? Who will call whom? Who will find the will? Where will the service be? Who will participate? Answering these and many other questions enables a family to work together for a common purpose that gives strength and encouragement.

The most appropriate liturgical signs of ministry with the dying include the richest rituals of the church: baptism and Holy Communion. Other rituals include anointing with holy oil in a Ministry with the Sick, praying The Sinner's Prayer, or offering an Act of Reconciliation.

✠ *Baptism or Baptismal Reaffirmation*

The Baptismal Covenant, the initiatory sign of a Christian's incorporation into the church, may be celebrated for the first time in the life of the person dying or reaffirmed for those persons who have been baptized previously.

This baptismal ministry extends to children as well as adults. Especially when a child is born critically ill or with a life-threatening condition, parents and family may wish for the child to be baptized immediately. Pastors may even be asked to baptize a stillborn child. Some families, who believe in adult baptism only, may ask for a child to be "dedicated." Many baptismal prayers may be used at such a time.

While ideally a child is baptized in a worshiping congregation, times of crisis call for pastoral ministry of the highest kind. Many maternity wards and chaplain's units in hospitals have emergency baptismal kits, which include a bowl, towel, and baptismal certificate. The hospital may also provide a Memory Box in which to put a lock of the child's hair or an impression of a footprint or handprint.

If the person dying has not been baptized, all that is required is for a youth or adult to accept Jesus Christ as Savior and be anointed with water in the name of the Trinity. Historically, any person may baptize either a child or an adult in such moments.

If the dying person has been baptized, an act of reaffirmation—laying on of hands, anointing the person with water, and offering prayer—witnesses to all people that the person through baptism is united with Christ in death and life.

In either case, the pastor may take a small bowl or cup of water, bless the water with a Trinitarian Prayer of Thanksgiving Over the Water, and either baptize or reaffirm the baptismal covenant by anointing the dying and others with the sign of the cross. The pastor places hands on or over the water. The pastor may either read the following Prayer of Thanksgiving Over the Water or pray extemporaneously:

Eternal God:
when nothing existed but chaos,

you swept across the dark waters
and brought forth light.
In the days of Noah
you saved those on the ark through water.
When you saw your people as slaves in Egypt,
you led them to freedom through the sea.
Their children you brought through the Jordan
to the land which you promised.

In the fullness of time you sent Jesus,
nurtured in the water of a womb.
Jesus was baptized by John and anointed by your Spirit.
Jesus called his disciples
to share in the baptism of his death and resurrection
and to make disciples of all nations.

Pour out your Holy Spirit,
to bless this gift of water and those who receive it,
especially this your servant,
Name of the dying *and others,*
to wash away their sin
and clothe them in righteousness,
that, dying and being raised with Christ,
they may share in his final victory. Amen.
(United Methodist, alt.)

At the end of the Prayer of Thanksgiving Over the Water, the pastor may sprinkle or pour water on the candidate or anoint the person with water, praying:

Name of the person, *I baptize you*
in the name of the Father, and the Son,
and the Holy Spirit.

Or

Name of the person, *I baptize you*
in the name of our Creator, Redeemer, and Sustainer.

Then the pastor lays hands on the head of the person dying and says a prayer. Other persons, including other persons present, may join the pastor in this action. During the laying on of hands, the pastor may pray:

Name of the dying,
> *the Holy Spirit work within you,*
> *that having been born through water and the Spirit,*
> *you may celebrate life everlasting*
> *with our Savior Jesus Christ. Amen.*

The pastor may also trace on the forehead of the dying and each person the sign of the cross in silence or with the words:

Name of the dying,
> *you are sealed and marked by the Holy Spirit*
> *as Christ's own child forever.*

⊕ *Holy Communion*

Holy Communion invokes the presence of Jesus Christ who lived, died, and lives again. We remember that Jesus on Easter appeared to two grieving followers at a breaking of the bread in Emmaus (Luke 24). Typically, the pastor brings both the bread and wine or fruit of the grapevine to the home, hospice, or hospital.

The service has four primary actions: taking the bread and cup, blessing the bread and cup, breaking the bread, and sharing the signs of Christ's presence. The elements of Holy Communion may be prepared, placing the bread and wine in a small communion set or simply a chalice (cup) and paten (plate). The pastor blesses the bread and cup with a Prayer of Great Thanksgiving. The bread is broken. Finally, the bread and cup are served with everyone who wishes to receive. If the dying person is not able to receive both the bread and cup, just a taste of the cup or a very small piece of bread is sufficient. Be sure to include caregivers and medical staff if they wish to participate.

The pastor may use the following abbreviated Prayer of Great Thanksgiving to God or offer a prayer extemporaneously:

> *It is right,*
> *that we should always and everywhere,*
> *and especially in times of life and death,*
> *give thanks to you, Almighty God,*
> *who breathed into us the breath of life.*
> *Holy are you, and blessed is your Son Jesus Christ.*
> *By the baptism of Jesus Christ's*
> *suffering, death, and resurrection*
> *you gave birth to your Church,*
> *delivered us from slavery to sin and death.*
>
> *On the night in which Jesus Christ gave himself up for*
> *us, he took bread,*
> *gave thanks to you, broke the bread,*
> *gave it to his disciples,*
> *and said:*

"Take, eat; this is my body which is given for you.
Do this in remembrance of me."

When the supper was over Jesus Christ took the cup,
    gave thanks to you, gave it to his disciples, and said:
"Drink from this, all of you;
    this is my blood of the new covenant,
    poured out for you
    and for many for the forgiveness of sins.
Do this, as often as you drink it, in remembrance of me."

In remembrance of these your mighty acts
in Jesus Christ,
    we offer ourselves as a holy and living sacrifice,
    in union with Christ's offering for us,
as we proclaim the mystery of faith:
    Christ has died;
    Christ is risen;
    Christ will come again.
Pour out your Holy Spirit on us, gathered here,
    and on these gifts of bread and wine.
Make them be for us the body and blood of Christ,
    that we may be for Name of the dying
    the body of Christ, who rose victorious from the dead,
    and comforts us with the blessed hope
    of everlasting life.

By your Spirit make us one with Christ,
    one with each other,
    and one in communion with all your saints,
    especially Names of others who have died
    whom we now remember in the silence of our hearts.

Observe a brief time of silence for thanksgiving and remembrance.

Finally, by your grace, bring Name of the dying
and all of us to that table

where your saints feast forever in your heavenly home.
Through your Son Jesus Christ,
with the Holy Spirit in your holy Church,
    all honor and glory is yours, almighty God,
    now and for ever. Amen.
(United Methodist, alt.)

✛ *Ministry with the Sick*

When someone is sick unto death, specific ministries of healing with the sick tradition may be used. This revised act may be used with or without Holy Communion, a Baptismal Reaffirmation, or An Act of Reconciliation.

Laying on of hands, anointing with oil, and the less formal gesture of holding someone's hand all show the power of touch, which plays a central role in the healings recorded in the New Testament. Jesus often touched others—blessing children, washing feet, healing injuries or disease, and raising people from death. Biblical precedent combines with our natural desire to reach out to persons in need in prompting us to touch gently and lovingly those who ask for healing prayers. Such an act is a tangible expression of the presence of the healing Christ, working in and through those who minister in his name.

Anointing the forehead with oil is a sign act invoking the healing love of God. The oil points beyond itself and those doing the anointing to the action of the Holy Spirit and the presence of the healing Christ, who is God's Anointed One. Olive oil is traditionally used in anointing, but it can become rancid. Sweet oil, which is olive oil with a preservative, is available in any pharmacy. Fragrant oils may be used, but care must be taken because some people are allergic to perfumes.

The pastor may begin by reading Scripture such as:

2 Corinthians 1:3-5	God comforts us in affliction.
Psalm 91	God will give angels charge.
Psalm 103	God forgives all your sins.
James 5:14-16	Is any among you sick?
Psalm 23 (page 70)	You have anointed my head with oil.
Mark 6:7, 12-13	They anointed with oil many that were sick.
1 John 5:13-15	That you may know that you have eternal life.

After any Scripture, the pastor may comment on it briefly.

Prayers may be offered.

The pastor may suggest the making of a special confession if the sick person's conscience is troubled. See "An Act of Reconciliation" on page 25.

The pastor may bless oil, using the following:

O Lord, holy Father, giver of health and salvation:
Send your Holy Spirit to sanctify this oil;
that, as your holy apostles anointed many
that were sick and healed them,
so may those who in faith and repentance
receive this holy oil
be made whole; through Jesus Christ our Lord,
who lives and reigns with you and the Holy Spirit,
one God, for ever and ever. Amen.

The pastor then lays hands upon the sick person, or if oil is used dips a thumb in the holy oil and makes the sign of the cross on the sick person's forehead, saying:

Name of the sick,
I lay my hands upon you or I anoint you with oil
in the Name of the Father, and of the Son,
and of the Holy Spirit,
asking our Lord Jesus Christ
to sustain you with his presence,
to drive away all sickness of body and spirit,
and to give you that victory of life and peace
that will enable you to serve God
both now and evermore. Amen.

The pastor concludes:

The Almighty Lord,
who is a strong tower to all who put their trust in him,

to whom all things in heaven, on earth,
   and under the earth bow and obey:
Be now and evermore your defense,
   and make you know and feel
   that the only Name under heaven given for health
   and salvation is the Name of our Lord Jesus Christ.
   Amen.
(United Methodist and Anglican, alt.)

✟ *The Sinner's Prayer*

The Sinner's Prayer, a short and simple plea for salvation, is a prayer of repentance for persons who feel convicted of the presence of sin in their life and seek the forgiveness of Jesus Christ. In some evangelical traditions, the prayer is the simple and necessary entry into a new relationship with Jesus Christ. Sometimes, a dying person or a family member may ask to pray the Sinner's Prayer as an act of assurance when death seems imminent. A number of versions of the prayer exist; the following is just one that may be shared by the pastor and repeated by the dying:

Heavenly Father, I know that I have sinned.
My sins have separated me from you.
   I am truly sorry
and want to follow a new path.
Forgive me.
I also believe in your Son Jesus Christ,
   who died for my sins
   and rose to new life.
I invite Jesus to be my Savior.
I will follow him
   and live as his disciple,
   both now and forever.
Now open for me
   the doors of heaven.
In Jesus' name I pray. Amen.

✝ *An Act of Reconciliation*

The ministry of reconciliation, out of the Roman Catholic and Anglican traditions, is another way to care for persons and their loved ones as death approaches. In this ritual, persons confess their sins and receive absolution/forgiveness. Such confessions may be heard anytime, but in times of death the need may become stronger.

Typically, the person confessing and the one hearing the confession, the confessor, sit close together. The penitent confesses one's sins. The one hearing the sins may suggest a psalm, prayer, or other act as a sign of penitence. The confession is not a subject to be discussed further, and for a pastor the content of the confession may never be shared.

The penitent person begins:

> *Bless me, for I have sinned.*

The pastor says:

> *The Lord be in your heart and upon your lips*
>   *that you may truly and humbly confess your sins:*
> *in the Name of the Father, and of the Son,*
>   *and of the Holy Spirit. Amen.*

Penitent (repeating after the pastor):

> *I confess to Almighty God,*
> *to God's Church,*
> *and to you,*
>   *that I have sinned by my own fault*
>   *in thought, word, and deed,*
>   *in things done and left undone;*
>   *especially _____.*
> *For these and all other sins*
> *which I cannot now remember,*
>   *I am truly sorry.*

I pray God to have mercy on me.
I firmly intend amendment of life,
   and I humbly beg forgiveness of God
   and God's Church,
   and ask you for counsel, direction, and absolution.

Here the pastor may offer counsel, direction, and comfort. The pastor then pronounces forgiveness:

Our Lord Jesus Christ,
   who has left power to his Church
   to absolve all sinners
   who truly repent and believe in him,
   of Christ's great mercy forgive you all your offenses;
and by his authority committed to me,
   I forgive you from all your sins:
in the Name of the Father, and of the Son,
and of the Holy Spirit. Amen. (Anglican, alt.)

Scriptures for the Dying and Persons with Life-threatening Illness

The following Scriptures may be read during a visit with the dying:

Psalm 23 (page 70)	The Lord is my shepherd.
Psalm 42	My soul longs for you.
Lamentations 3:22-23	The steadfast love of God
Ecclesiastes 3:1-11a (page 79)	For everything there is a season.
Isaiah 25:6-10	God will swallow up death.
Isaiah 61:1-3	The Spirit of the Lord
Romans 8:18-25 (page 85)	Present sufferings and future glory
Romans 14:7-9	We are the Lord's.

✠ *Prayers with the Dying*

As the pastor visits with the dying, the Lord's Prayer (see page 117) or Psalm 23 (see page 70) may be led by the pastor and joined by others as they are able.

Prayer with a person with a life-threatening illness:

Lord Jesus Christ,
  we come to you sharing
  the suffering that you endured.
Grant us patience during this time,
  that as we and Name of the dying
  live with pain, disappointment, and frustration,
we may realize that suffering is a part of life,
  a part of life that you know intimately.
Touch Name of the dying *in* his/her *time of trial,*
  hold him/her *tenderly in your loving arms,*
  and let him/her *know you care.*
Renew us in our spirits,
  even when our bodies are not being renewed,
that we might be ever prepared to dwell
  in your eternal home,
  through our faith in you, Lord Jesus,
  who died and are alive for evermore. Amen.
(United Methodist)

Prayers with a person in a coma or unable to communicate:

Eternal God, you have known us before we were here
  and will continue to know us after we are gone.
Touch Name of the dying *with your grace and presence.*
As you give your abiding care,
  assure him/her *of our love and presence.*

28

Assure him/her *that our communion together
    remains secure,
    and that your love for* him/her *is unfailing.
In Christ, who came to us, we pray. Amen.
(United Methodist)*

Prayers for a person near death:

*Almighty God, look on this your servant,
    lying in great weakness,
    and comfort* Name of the dying
    *with the promise of life everlasting,
given in the resurrection
of your Son Jesus Christ our Lord. Amen. (Anglican)*

Lord Jesus Christ, deliver your child and servant,
Name of the dying,
    *from all evil
    and set* him/her *free from every bond;
    that* he/she *may rest with all your saints
    in the joy of your eternal home, for ever and ever.
Amen. (United Methodist, alt.)*

Go forward, Name of the dying,
    *on your pilgrim journey,
in the name of the Father who created you;
in the name of Jesus Christ who died and rose for you;
in the name of the Holy Spirit who strengthens you.
May you have communion with all the saints in light;
    may you rejoice with the whole company of heaven;
    may your portion this day be peace,
    and your dwelling place the heavenly Jerusalem.
Amen. (Australian)*

*Gracious God, you are nearer than hands or feet,
    closer than breathing.*

Sustain with your presence our brother/sister
   Name of the dying.
Help him/her *now to trust in your goodness*
     and claim your promise of life everlasting.
Cleanse him/her *of all sin and remove all burdens.*
Grant him/her *the sure joy of your salvation,*
     through Jesus Christ our Lord. Amen.
(Presbyterian)

CHAPTER THREE

MINISTRY IMMEDIATELY FOLLOWING DEATH

When a person dies, the pastor often gathers with family and others beside the bed of the deceased. The pastor now focuses attention on the family, caregivers, and others who are present. The pastor may pray extemporaneously or pray one or more of the Commendation and Final Prayers (see page 119), or the following prayers:

When a life-support system is withdrawn:

> *O God, you are the Alpha and Omega,*
> *the beginning and the end.*
> *You breathed into us the breath of life,*
> *and watched over us all our days.*
> *Now, in time of death, we return*
> Name of the deceased *to you,*
> *trusting in your steadfast love,*
> *through Jesus Christ our Savior. Amen.*
> *(United Methodist)*

At the time of death, the pastor may lay hands (and invite others to join in this act) on the head of the dying person, and pray one or more of the following:

Depart in peace, brother/sister Name of the deceased;
   in the name of God the Father who created you;
   in the name of Christ who redeemed you;
   in the name of the Holy Spirit who sanctifies you.
May you rest in peace, and dwell for ever with the Lord.
Amen. (United Methodist)

Almighty God, our Creator and Redeemer,
you have given us our brother/sister Name of deceased,
   to know and to love in our pilgrimage on earth.
Uphold us now as we entrust him/her
   to your boundless love and eternal care.
Assure us that not even death can separate us
   from your infinite mercy.
Deal graciously with us who mourn,
   that we may truly know your sure consolation
   and learn to live in confident hope of the Resurrection;
through your Son, Jesus Christ our Lord. Amen.
(Presbyterian)

Out of the depths we cry to you, O Lord.
Hear our voice.
We wait for you, O God. Our souls wait for you.
Give us now your word of hope.
We know your love is steadfast,
   always there when we need it.
Let us feel your presence now in our time of sorrow.
Help us to look to tomorrow to see hope beyond grief,
   through Jesus Christ our Lord. Amen.
(United Methodist)

Depart, O Christian soul, out of this world;
   in the Name of God the Father Almighty
   who created you;
   in the Name of Jesus Christ who redeemed you;
   in the Name of the Holy Spirit who sanctifies you.

May your rest be this day in peace,
and your dwelling place in the Paradise of God.
(Anglican)

Lord Jesus,
we wait for you to grant us your comfort and peace.
We confess that we are slow to accept death
as an inevitable part of life.
We confess our reluctance to surrender
this friend and loved one into your eternal care.
You, Lord Jesus, know the depth of our sorrow;
you also wept at the grave of your friend Lazarus.
Let the Holy Spirit come upon us now,
the Comforter you promised.
Grant us your love and peace
as we reach out to comfort one another.
Be our companion as we live through the days ahead;
and even as we mourn,
may all that we feel, think, say, and do
bear witness to our Faith. Amen. (Australian)

After the death of a child:

Loving God,
as your son Jesus took children into his arms
and blessed the children,
give us grace to entrust Name of the child
into your steadfast love,
through Jesus Christ our Savior. Amen.
(United Methodist)

After the birth of a stillborn child or the death of a newly born child, pray
for the mother, father, or other family members or caregivers:

Merciful God, you strengthen us
by your power and wisdom.

33

Be gracious to Name(s) of family *in their grief*
and surround them with your unfailing love;
that they may not be overwhelmed by their loss
but have confidence in your goodness,
and courage to meet the days to come;
through Jesus Christ our Lord. Amen. (Australian)

For a victim of a crime:

Lord God of liberation,
you saw your people as slaves in Egypt
and delivered them from captivity,
you see works of violence and weep.
Relieve the suffering of Name of the victim,
grant him/her *peace.*
Grant all of us a renewed faith in your protection and care.
Protect us all from the violence of others,
keep us safe from the weapons of hate,
and restore us to tranquility and peace.
We ask this through Christ our Lord. Amen.
(Roman Catholic, alt.)

Scriptures for a victim of a crime:

Job 3:1-26	Lamentation of Job
Isaiah 59:6b-8, 15b-18	God appalled by evil and injustice
Lamentations 3:1-24	One who knows affliction
Lamentations 3:49-59	You come to my aid.
Matthew 5:1-10	The Beatitudes
Matthew 10:28-31	Do not be afraid.

Litany at the time of death. When possible, members of the family and friends may join together in the following litany:

God the Father, **have mercy on your servant.**
God the Son, **have mercy on your servant.**

God the Holy Spirit, **have mercy on your servant.**
Holy Trinity, one God, **have mercy on your servant.**
From all evil, from all sin, from all tribulation,
   Good Lord, deliver Name of the dying.
By your holy Incarnation, by your Cross and Passion,
   by your precious Death and Burial,
   Good Lord, deliver your servant.
By your glorious Resurrection and Ascension,
   and by the Coming of the Holy Spirit,
   Good Lord, deliver your servant.
We sinners beseech you to hear us, Lord Christ:
   that it may please you to deliver
   the soul of your servant
   from the power of evil, and from eternal death,
   we beseech you to hear us, good Lord.
That it may please you mercifully to pardon
   all his/her *sins,*
   we beseech you to hear us, good Lord.
That it may please you to grant him/her
   a place of refreshment
   and everlasting blessedness,
   we beseech you to hear us, good Lord.
That it may please you to give him/her
   joy and gladness in your kingdom,
   with your saints in light,
   we beseech you to hear us, good Lord.
Jesus, Lamb of God: **have mercy on your servant.**
Jesus, bearer of our sins: **have mercy on your servant.**
Jesus, redeemer of the world:
   give your servant your peace.
Lord, have mercy.
   Christ, have mercy.
Lord, have mercy.
(Anglican)

CHAPTER FOUR

A FAMILY HOUR, WAKE, OR VIGIL

Family and friends often gather for sharing and prayers in the church, funeral home, or family home on the day or night before a funeral or memorial service, or just before the service itself. Many times, the deceased's body is in an open casket, clothed in the deceased's finest clothes and jewelry. In the presence of the deceased, persons greet one another and friends offer support to the bereaved.

Families may also display pictures, special belongings of the deceased, and other items to honor and remember the deceased. Persons also often sign a book or register condolences online. Other names for this time include Visitation, Calling Hours, and Viewing.

While the occasion may be primarily social, with many informal conversations, a family may also wish for a period of more focused sharing in which everyone shares stories. Everyone listens to persons who may not feel comfortable speaking at a more formal funeral or memorial service.

The following pattern offers a service of remembrance and thanksgiving for the deceased and comfort for the bereaved. This service may be quite informal. After a time of greetings and condolences exchanged by family and friends informally or with receiving lines, the service begins. Acts of worship from throughout this book may be included or substituted for those below. The coffin may be open or closed, depending on the wishes of the family.

Either pastors or laypersons may lead this service.

In the Roman Catholic tradition, the service may be preceded or followed by a rosary service when additional prayers are offered for the deceased and grieving family.

If the deceased is a member of a fraternal or other organization that customarily holds services for its deceased members, the organization may wish to conduct a special service according to its customs before or after this time. For example, members of civic clubs, firefighters, military personnel, and police all have distinct ways of honoring their deceased. Plans for such services should be made in consultation with the family and pastor. See pages 11-12 for more details.

✠ *Greetings*

The pastor or other person may open with a short Opening Prayer (see page 46) or with a brief greeting or introductory statement on behalf of the church, family, and friends, such as:

Friends, we are gathered here
  to honor the memory of our departed friend and
  brother/sister, Name of the deceased.

✠ *Hymns*

One or more stanzas of a well-known hymn or song may be sung or recited. See pages 52-56 for suggestions.

✠ *Prayers*

The leader or some other person may pray an extemporaneous prayer, or the following or another prayer (see Opening Prayers on page 57):

Gracious God,
  as your Son wept with Mary and Martha
  at the tomb of Lazarus,

look with compassion on those who grieve,
especially Names of family and friends.
Grant them the assurance of your presence now
and faith in your eternal goodness,
that in them may be fulfilled the promise
that those who mourn shall be comforted;
through Jesus Christ our Lord. Amen. (United Methodist)

✛ *Scriptures*

One of the following Scriptures may be read. Also consider the other Scriptures included on pages 70-101:

Psalm 23 (page 70)	The Lord is my shepherd.
Psalm 27	The Lord is my light.
Psalm 90:1-6, 12, 16-17	From everlasting to everlasting
Psalm 121	I lift up my eyes to the hills.
John 14:1-10a, 15-21, 25-27	Do not let your hearts be
(page 92)	troubled.

✛ *Witness*

Family, friends, and members of the congregation may briefly voice their thankfulness to God for the grace they have received in the life of the deceased and their Christian faith and joy. Stories, shared experiences, and humor are appropriate. Persons may also offer support for other family members and friends, as words of faith, hope, and love are exchanged. See pages 104-6 for more commentary about the time of Witness and Naming.

✛ *Closing Prayers and Blessings*

The following prayer from Numbers 6:24-26 (alt.) or another Commendation or Final Prayer (see pages 119-22) may be spoken. If the litany below is used, pass out copies to enable everyone to participate:

The Lord bless us and keep us.
The Lord make his face to shine upon us
and be gracious to us.

The Lord lift up his countenance upon us
  and give us peace. Amen. (United Methodist)

Dear Friends: It was our Lord Jesus himself who said,
  "Come to me, all you who labor and are burdened,
  and I will give you rest."
Let us pray, then, for our brother/sister,
  Name of the deceased,
  that he/she *may rest from* his/her *labors,*
and enter into the light of God's eternal sabbath rest.

Receive, O Lord, your servant, for he/she *returns to you.*
Into your hands, O Lord,
  we commend our brother/sister, Name of the deceased.
Wash him/her *in the holy font of everlasting life,*
  and clothe him/her *in* his/her
  heavenly wedding garment.
Into your hands, O Lord,
  we commend our brother/sister, Name of the deceased.
May he/she *hear your words of invitation,*
  "Come, you blessed of my Father."
Into your hands, O Lord,
  we commend our brother/sister, Name of the deceased.
May he/she *gaze upon you, Lord, face to face,*
  and taste the blessedness of perfect rest.
Into your hands, O Lord,
  we commend our brother/sister, Name of the deceased.
May angels surround him/her,
  and saints welcome him/her *in peace.*
Into your hands, O Lord,
  we commend our brother/sister, Name of the deceased.
Almighty God, our Father in heaven,
  before whom live all who die in the Lord:
Receive our brother/sister, Name of the deceased
  into the courts of your heavenly dwelling place.
Let his/her *heart and soul now ring out in joy to you,*
  O Lord, the living God, and the God of those who live.
This we ask through Christ our Lord. Amen. (Anglican, alt.)

CHAPTER FIVE

SERVICES OF DEATH AND RESURRECTION (FUNERALS AND MEMORIAL SERVICES)

The following resources may be used in any service of worship to honor the dead.

Keep the service tight, focused, and deliberate. It is always better for persons to wish that a service had been longer than shorter. Less is more in many funerals.

This resource includes many prayers and Scriptures; pick the ones that best fit the needs of a particular person and family. Not every act of worship included here is needed every time.

The most basic purpose of Christian worship is to proclaim the good news of Jesus Christ's death and resurrection through the reading of God's Holy Word. The Scriptures may be read in any order, although they are listed in this resource in the order that they are often read in Sunday worship: Old Testament, Psalms, Epistles, and Gospels.

These services do not always need a psalm, and an Old Testament reading, and an Epistle lesson, and a Gospel text. The Scriptures included in this resource are those most recommended historically and most often used. Yet, in general, a few longer texts carefully, quietly, and prayerfully offered are superior to a longer sermon. Trust the Word of God in the Bible to speak.

Carefully read the Scriptures, especially those texts that are presumed to be known by everyone, clearly, slowly, and passionately. Pastors should practice reading them as the direct Word of God for the people of God.

After the service has been planned, walk through the movements of the worship mentally before the service begins. Make sure that the choreography of the service flows smoothly. When will each participant speak or sing? When will people stand or sit? Where does the music best fit? When is there a time for silence? Where will people sit? Can every action be seen and every word heard?

Prepare an outline or worship bulletin of the service and give a copy to each musician, participant, the funeral director, and others assisting with the service.

A complete bulletin with every element listed would include:

A Service of Death and Resurrection, Name of the Deceased

Location	**Creed*
Time	*Prayer of Thanksgiving*
Gathering Music	*The Lord's Prayer*
Words of Grace	** Hymn*
*Entrance Hymn	** Commendation*
Greeting	** Dismissal with Blessing*
Opening Prayer	*The service will continue with a*
Psalm	*Committal at . . .*
Old Testament	*The family will receive friends . . .*
Epistle	*Service Participants:*
Solo	*Musician*
New Testament	*Witness*
Witnesses	*Pastor*
*Hymn	*The obituary downloaded and*
Eulogy	*printed.*

✤ *Entrance and Gathering*

Before the service begins, the pastor has final responsibility for the worship space. Adjust the heat or air conditioning. Turn on the lights. Arrange the right paraments. Reserve the correct pews for family, pallbearers, and others. Turn on the sound system. Set the flowers in the right place. Be sure that the musicians and other worship leaders know their roles. Finally, light the candles.

The family may have gathered before the service for a meal and time of remembrance. The family may also have had one final opportunity to see the body before the casket is closed, and the pastor may be asked to pray in that moment. In Greek Orthodox services, the family may also be given the opportunity to see the body one last time after the service is over.

As the congregation gathers, the family and close friends may gather outside the sanctuary to prepare for a procession. The pastor may greet both the congregation and the family. As the congregation and family arrive, a calm, warm welcome and hug by the pastor assures everyone that the service is in good hands.

Music may be offered while the family and congregation gather. The music sets the tone of the funeral as the people focus their thoughts. The music may include beloved hymns on a piano or organ or other musical instrument. Recorded music loved by the deceased may also be played.

Hymns and songs of faith may also be sung during the gathering by the congregation. See the suggestions for hymns on pages 52-56.

Church bells may be rung as the casket and family arrive at the church.

The coffin or urn may be covered with a pall before the procession. The pall, a large cloth with a simple cross or elaborate symbols, reminds us that Christians are clothed by Jesus Christ in baptism; thus the saying: "As in baptism *Name of the deceased* put on Christ, so in Christ may *Name of the deceased* be clothed with glory."

Often the pall is white, with accents and symbols in gold, red, or green. The pall also signifies the equality of all members as it covers the casket, preventing persons from wondering about the cost of the casket. Flowers are never put on top of the pall. In many congregations, the pall is placed over the casket as it comes into the church building. Alternatively, the coffin may be covered with a national flag, or with a large spray of flowers.

As the service begins, the coffin or urn may be carried into the place of worship in procession by the pallbearers, family, or friends. The procession is an important act of worship, giving respect to the family and honor to the deceased. Even in a funeral home, include a procession to honor the deceased.

Invite the congregation to stand as one is able. A member of the congregation or acolyte, bearing a lighted Paschal candle, may lead the procession into the church. Traditionally, the pastor goes first, followed by the casket, and then the family.

The family is seated near the coffin and in sight of the congregation. Thankfully, an older tradition of separating the family from the sight of the congregation, to allow the family to grieve separately, has mostly been abandoned. When the family is seated, then the pastor invites all to be seated.

Typically, the coffin remains closed throughout the service, although families may choose otherwise. Traditionally, the head of the coffin is away from the Altar/table, except in the case of clergy, when the head is toward the Altar/table. Or, the casket is simply placed where it is most easily seen by the whole congregation. If Holy Communion will be celebrated, be sure that the placement of the casket does not interfere with the serving of the Holy Meal.

As the pall is placed, or as the procession begins when the pall is not used, the pastor may offer one or more of the following, either just with the family or for the whole congregation. These statements may also be used at the Words of Grace (in front of the whole congregation after the casket/urn is in place):

Dying, Christ destroyed our death.
Rising, Christ restored our life.
Christ will come again in glory.
As in baptism Name of the deceased *put on Christ,*

so in Christ may Name of the deceased
be clothed with glory.

Here and now, dear friends, we are God's children.
What we shall be has not yet been revealed;
   but we know that when Christ appears,
   we shall be like our Savior,
   for we shall see Christ as he is.
Those who have this hope purify themselves
   as Christ is pure. (United Methodist, alt.)

With faith in Jesus Christ,
   we receive the body of our brother/sister,
   Name of the deceased *for burial.*
Let us pray with confidence to God, the Giver of life,
   that God will raise him/her
   to perfection in the company of the saints.

Silence may be kept; after which the pastor prays:

Deliver your servant, Name of the deceased,
   O Sovereign Lord Christ, from all evil,
   and set him/her *free from every bond;*
   that he/she *may rest with all your saints*
   in the eternal habitations;
where with the Father and the Holy Spirit
you live and reign,
   one God, for ever and ever. Amen.
Let us also pray for all who mourn,
   that they may cast their care on God,
   and know the consolation of God's love.

Silence may be kept; after which the pastor prays:

Almighty God, look with pity
   upon the sorrows of your servants for whom we pray.

Remember them, Lord, in your mercy;
    nourish them with patience;
    comfort them with a sense of your goodness;
lift up your countenance upon them;
    and give them peace; through Jesus Christ our Lord.
    Amen. (Anglican, alt.)

✛ *Words of Grace*

The Words of Grace are the first proclamation to the congregation of the presence of Jesus Christ, the living Word of God, and the holy mystery of Christ's victory over sin and death.

If the coffin or urn is carried into the place of worship in procession, the pastor may go before the casket or urn speaking these Words of Grace. Typically, except in Orthodox funerals, the casket is closed. Or, following the procession when the coffin or urn is already in place, the pastor speaks from in front of the congregation, which may still be standing, one or more of the following:

Jesus said, I am the resurrection and I am life.
Those who believe in me, even though they die,
    yet shall they live,
    and whoever lives and believes in me shall never die.
I am Alpha and Omega, the beginning and the end,
    the first and the last.
I died, and behold I am alive for evermore,
    and I hold the keys of hell and death.
Because I live, you shall live also. (United Methodist)

The eternal God is your dwelling place,
    and underneath are the everlasting arms.
(Deuteronomy 33:27, alt.)

The Lord is my light and my salvation;
    whom shall I fear?
The Lord is the stronghold of my life;
    of whom shall I be afraid? (Psalm 27:1)

Blessed be the Lord,
    who has heard the voice of my supplications!
The Lord is my strength and shield,
    in whom my heart trusts. (Psalm 28:6-7a, alt.)

God is our refuge and strength,
    a very present help in trouble. (Psalm 46:1)

The Lord is merciful and gracious,
    slow to anger and abounding in steadfast love.
As a father shows compassion to his children,
    so the Lord shows compassion to the faithful.
For the Lord knows our frame,
    and remembers that we are dust.
The steadfast love of the Lord
    is from everlasting to everlasting
    upon the faithful,
and the righteousness of the Lord to children's children.
(Psalm 103:8, 13-14, 17)

Come to me, all you that are weary
    and are carrying heavy burdens,
and I will give you rest. (Matthew 11:28)

The Lamb at the center of the throne
    will be their shepherd,
    and the Lamb will guide the saints
    to springs of the water of life,
    and God will wipe away every tear from their eyes.
(Revelation 7:17, alt.)

Jesus said:
    Do not be afraid,
    I am the first and the last,
    and the living one;
    I was dead, and behold, I am alive forever and ever.
(Revelation 1:17-18)

As for me, I know that my Redeemer lives
    and that at the last he will stand upon the earth.
After my awaking, my Redeemer will raise me up;
    and in my body I shall see God.
I myself shall see, and my eyes behold God
    who is my friend and not a stranger.
For none of us has life in ourselves,

47

and none becomes our own master when we die.
For if we have life, we are alive in the Lord,
and if we die, we die in the Lord.
So, then, whether we live or die,
we are the Lord's possession.
Happy from now on
are those who die in the Lord!
So it is, says the Spirit,
for they rest from their labors. (Anglican, alt.)

When we were baptized in Christ Jesus,
we were baptized into his death.
We were buried therefore with Christ
by baptism into death,
so that as Christ was raised from the dead
by the glory of the Father,
we too might live a new life.
For if we have been united with Christ
in a death like his,
we shall certainly be united with Christ
in a resurrection like his. (Lutheran, alt.)

At the Service for a Child, the following may be used:

Jesus said: "Truly I tell you, unless you change
and become like children,
you will never enter the kingdom of heaven.
Whoever becomes humble like this child
is the greatest in the kingdom of heaven.
Take care that you do not despise
one of these little ones;
for, I tell you,
in heaven their angels continually see
the face of my Father in heaven.
So it is not the will of your Father in heaven
that one of these little ones should be lost."
(Matthew 18:3-4, 10, 14)

Jesus said: "Let the little children come to me,
    and do not stop them;
for it is to such as these
    that the kingdom of heaven belongs."
(Matthew 19:14)

And Jesus took the children up in his arms,
    laid his hands on them, and blessed them.
(Mark 10:16, alt.)

For an untimely or tragic death:

Blessed be the God who consoles us in all our affliction,
so that we may be able to console those
    who are in any affliction
    with the consolation
    with which we ourselves are consoled by God.
(2 Corinthians 1:3a, 4)

Cast your burden on the Lord, and God will sustain you.
(Psalm 55:22a, alt.)

For a person who did not profess the Christian faith: if the faith of the deceased or of the mourners is such that the pastor considers traditional acts inappropriate, adaptations may be made with appropriate consultation so that no one's integrity is violated. The acts of worship throughout this book may not be appropriate for persons who were active adherents of other religions.

The Lord is near to the brokenhearted,
    and saves the crushed in spirit. (Psalm 34:18)

The Lord heals the brokenhearted,
    and binds up their wounds.
Great is our Lord, and abundant in power,
    whose understanding is beyond measure.
(Psalm 147:3, 5)

✛ Greetings

The people are seated. The pastor continues by welcoming the congregation and announcing the purpose of the service, where both grief and faith are proclaimed. The pastor uses one or more of the following:

Friends, we have gathered here to praise God
    and to witness to our faith as we celebrate
    the life of Name of the deceased.
We come together in grief, acknowledging our human loss.
May God grant us grace,
    that in pain we may find comfort,
    in sorrow hope, in death resurrection.
(United Methodist)

Welcome in the name of Jesus, the Savior of the world.
We are gathered to worship,
    to proclaim Christ crucified and risen,
    to remember before God
    our sister/brother Name of the deceased,
    to give thanks for her/his *life,*
    to commend her/him *to our merciful redeemer,*
    and to comfort one another in our grief. (Lutheran)

At the service for a child:

Friends, we have gathered to worship God
    and to witness to our faith
    even as we mourn the death of this infant
    or Name of child,
    and Names of the parents.
We come together in grief,
    acknowledging our human loss.
May God search our hearts,
    that in pain we may find comfort,
    in sorrow hope, in death resurrection.
(United Methodist, alt.)

For a stillborn child:

Friends, we have gathered here in our grief
to praise God and witness to our faith.
We come together in grief,
acknowledging our human loss of one so young.
He/She *has been given a name:* Name of the child,
with the Church's blessing.
May God grant us grace,
that in pain we may find comfort,
in sorrow hope, in death resurrection.
(United Methodist, alt.)

If not used before at the placing of the pall and the procession, the pastor may also say:

Dying, Christ destroyed our death.
Rising, Christ restored our life.
Christ will come again in glory.
As in baptism Name of the deceased *put on Christ,*
so in Christ may Name of the deceased
be clothed with glory.
(United Methodist)

✠ *Music, Hymns, and Songs*

Music and hymnody play a vital role in any service. The music may be somber or joyful or both. The opening voluntaries often set the mood for the entire service. Through musical instruments and human voices, persons are united with each other and with God.

Several guidelines are appropriate:

1. The music and texts should aid the flow of the service and not be a distraction or interruption. Use music throughout the service to reinforce the promise of life to the deceased and comfort for the bereaved.
2. Familiar music is usually best.
3. When the hymns and songs are known, instead of using a soloist or choir, invite the whole congregation to sing.
4. Soloists and choirs should assist, not dominate the service. The focus must always be on the deceased and grieving congregation, not the persons singing and their performance.
5. Many musical instruments may be appropriate, including piano, organ, trumpet, harp, violin, and bagpipe, among other instruments.
6. Instead of singing these hymns and songs, sometimes a simple playing of the instrumental music on organ, piano, or other instrument, especially of a familiar hymn, provides a time for silent reflection and remembrance.
7. When secular music is chosen, such as a favorite of the deceased, it is best for that music to be played before or after the service. This advice is particularly true if the song is recorded and simply broadcast.

There are also exceptions to all the above rules. A New Orleans tradition includes a somber funeral dirge, followed by celebrative music such as "When the Saints Go Marching In." Participants use upbeat music with "second line" dancing, where celebrants do a dance-march, to create a joyful celebration. Participants raise hats, wave handkerchiefs, and lift umbrellas (protection from the intense New Orleans weather).

One or more of the following hymns may be used throughout the service. Of particular interest are hymns that were beloved by the deceased. The pastor may wish to copy this list of hymns (and others) and provide the list to the family to help them in selecting the music for the service. Not all the verses of each selection need to be sung.

Abide with Me
Amazing Grace
Ask Ye What Great Thing I Know
Beams of Heaven As I Go
Blest Be the Tie that Binds
Children of the Heavenly Father
Christ Is Alive
Christ the Victorious
Close to Thee
Come, Let Us Join Our Friends Above
Come, Thou Long-Expected Jesus
Come, We That Love the Lord
Come, Ye Disconsolate
Come, Ye Faithful, Raise the Strain
Faith of Our Fathers
Fix Me, Jesus
For All the Saints
Give to the Winds Thy Fears
Glorious Things of Thee Are Spoken
Great Is Thy Faithfulness
He Leadeth Me: O Blessed Thought
How Blest Are They Who Trust in Christ
How Firm a Foundation
How Great Thou Art
Hymn of Promise (In the Bulb There Is a Flower)
I Am Thine, O Lord
I Sing a Song of the Saints of God
I'll Praise My Maker While I've Breath

Immortal, Invisible, God Only Wise
In the Garden
Jesus, Joy of Our Desiring
Jesus, Remember Me
Just As I Am, Without One Plea
Leaning on the Everlasting Arms
Marching to Zion
More Love to Thee
My Faith Looks Up to Thee
My Hope Is Built
Nearer, My God, to Thee
Nobody Knows the Trouble I See
O For a Thousand Tongues to Sing
O Day of Peace that Dimly Shines
O God, Our Help in Ages Past
O Love that Wilt Not Let Me Go
O Mary, Don't You Weep
O Morning Star, How Fair and Bright
O Thou, in Whose Presence
O What Their Joy and Their Glory Must Be
Of the Father's Love Begotten
On Eagle's Wings
On Jordan's Stormy Banks I Stand
Pues Si Vivimos (When We Are Living)
Praise, My Soul, the King of Heaven
Precious Lord, Take My Hand
Remember Me
Rejoice in God's Saints
Saranam, Saranam (Refuge)
Shalom to You
Shall We Gather at the River
Sing with All the Saints in Glory
Soon, and Very Soon
Stand by Me

Steal Away to Jesus
Sweet Hour of Prayer
Swing Low, Sweet Chariot
Take Time to Be Holy
The Church's One Foundation
The Day of Resurrection
The God of Abraham Praise
The Old Rugged Cross
There's a Wideness in God's Mercy
Thine Be the Glory
This Is a Day of New Beginnings
Thou Hidden Source of Calm Repose
'Tis So Sweet to Trust in Jesus
'Tis the Old Ship of Zion
To God Be the Glory
Up from the Grave He Arose
Victory in Jesus
We Shall Overcome
What a Friend We Have in Jesus
When We All Get to Heaven

Suggested Hymns for the Service for a Child
Children of the Heavenly Father
Hymn of Promise
Jesus Loves Me

Hymns for an Untimely or Tragic Death
Blest Be the Tie that Binds
Children of the Heavenly Father
Come, Ye Disconsolate
Give to the Winds Thy Fears
He Leadeth Me: O Blessed Thought
Hymn of Promise (especially for a youth)
My Faith Looks Up to Thee

55

Nearer, My God, to Thee
O God, Our Help in Ages Past
O Love that Wilt Not Let Me Go
Precious Lord, Take My Hand
Pues Si Vivimos (When We Are Living; especially for a young adult)
Thine Be the Glory (especially for a middle adult)
We'll Understand It Better By and By

✢ *Opening Prayers*

Funerals and memorial services may best be considered services of Scripture and prayer rather than sermon-centered worship. One or more of the following or other prayers may be offered, possibly in unison by the whole congregation. Each of these prayers focus on a different need, from a petition for God's help, to thanksgiving for the communion of saints, and to confession of sin with an assurance of pardon and are all appropriate depending on the service. Extemporaneous prayers and others forms of prayers are also appropriate. These prayers invite praying them slowly, with times of silence, so that persons may reflect upon their meaning.

A prayer for God's help:

O God, who gave us birth,
you are ever more ready to hear
than we are to pray.
You know our needs before we ask,
and our ignorance in asking.
Give to us now your grace,
that as we shrink before the mystery of death,
we may see the light of eternity.
Speak to us once more
your solemn message of life and of death.
Help us to live as those who are prepared to die.
And when our days here are accomplished,
enable us to die as those who go forth to live,
so that living or dying, our life may be in you,
and that nothing in life or in death
will be able to separate us
from your great love in Christ Jesus our Lord. Amen.
(United Methodist)

O God of grace and glory,
we remember before you today our sister/brother,

Name of the deceased.
We thank you for giving her/him *to us to know*
and to love as companion in our pilgrimage on earth.
In your boundless compassion,
console us who mourn.
Give us faith to see that death has been swallowed up
in the victory of our Lord Jesus Christ,
so that we may live in confidence and hope until,
by your call,
we are gathered to our heavenly home
In the company of all your saints;
through Jesus Christ, our Savior and Lord. Amen.
(Lutheran)

A prayer for strength:

Eternal God, our heavenly Father,
your love for us is everlasting
You alone can turn the shadow of death
into the brightness of the morning light.
By the power of the Holy Spirit,
come to us in our darkness and distress
with the light and peace of your presence.
Speak to us now through your holy word,
that our faith may be strengthened
and our hope sustained;
through Jesus Christ our Lord. Amen. (Australian)

A prayer of thanksgiving for the saints:

Eternal God,
we praise you for the great company of all those
who have finished their course in faith
and now rest from their labor.
We praise you for those dear to us
who have departed from this life, and
whom we now name in our hearts before you.

Leave a moment for silent prayer.

Especially we praise you for Name of the deceased,
whom you have graciously received into your presence.

Leave a moment for silent prayer.

To all of these who have departed, grant your peace.
Let perpetual light shine upon them;
and help us so to believe where we have not seen,
*   that your presence may lead us through our years,*
*   and bring us at last with them*
*   into the joy of your home*
*   not made with hands but eternal in the heavens;*
through Jesus Christ our Lord. Amen.
(United Methodist, alt.)

A prayer of comfort:

Eternal God, maker of heaven and earth:
*   You formed us from the dust of the earth,*
*   and by your breath you gave us life. We glorify you.*
Jesus Christ, the resurrection and the life:
*   You tasted death for all humanity,*
*   and by rising from the grave*
*   you opened the way to eternal life. We praise you.*
Holy Spirit, author and giver of life:
*   You are the comforter of all who sorrow,*
*   our sure confidence and everlasting hope.*
*   We worship you.*
To you, O blessed Trinity,
*   be glory and honor, forever and ever. Amen.*
(Presbyterian)

A prayer for assurance of God's presence:

O Jesus Christ our risen Lord,
you have gone before us in death.
Grant us the assurance of your presence,
that we who are anxious and fearful
in the face of death
may confidently face the future,
in the knowledge that you have prepared a place for
all who love you. Amen. (United Methodist)

A prayer for trust:

O God, giver of life and conqueror of death,
our help in every time of trouble,
we trust that you do not willingly grieve or afflict us.
Comfort us who mourn;
and give us grace, in the presence of death,
to worship you,
that we may have sure hope of eternal life
and be enabled to put our whole trust
in your goodness and mercy;
through Jesus Christ our Lord. Amen.
(United Methodist)

A prayer for refuge:

Almighty God, our Father, from whom we come,
and to whom our spirits return:
You have been our dwelling place in all generations.
You are our refuge and strength,
a very present help in trouble.
Grant us your blessing in this hour,
and enable us so to put our trust in you
that our spirits may grow calm
and our hearts be comforted.
Lift our eyes beyond the shadows of earth,
and help us to see the light of eternity.

So may we find grace and strength
for this and every time of need;
through Jesus Christ our Lord. Amen.
(United Methodist)

A prayer of thanks:

O God of grace and glory,
we remember before you this day our brother/sister,
Name of the deceased.
We thank you for giving him/her *to us,*
his/her *family and friends,*
to know and to love as a companion
on our earthly pilgrimage.
In your boundless compassion, console us who mourn.
Give us faith to see in death the gate of eternal life,
so that in quiet confidence we may continue
our course on earth, until, by your call,
we are reunited with those who have gone before;
through Jesus Christ our Lord. Amen. (Anglican)

A prayer for confidence:

O God, whose days are without end,
and whose mercies cannot be numbered:
Make us, we pray, deeply aware of the shortness
and uncertainty of human life;
and let your Holy Spirit lead us in holiness
and righteousness all our days;
that when we shall have served you in our generation,
we may be gathered to our ancestors,
having the testimony of a good conscience,
in the communion of the Catholic Church,
in the confidence of a certain faith,
in the comfort of a religious and holy hope,
in favor with you, our God,

and in perfect charity with the world.
All this we ask through Jesus Christ our Lord. Amen.
(Anglican)

A prayer for faith:

Lord Jesus Christ,
*   by your death you took away the sting of death:*
Grant to us your servants so to follow in faith
*   where you have led the way,*
*   that we may at length fall asleep peacefully in you*
*   and wake up in your likeness;*
for your tender mercies' sake. Amen. (Anglican)

A prayer for courage:

Grant, O Lord, to all who are bereaved
*   the spirit of faith and courage,*
*   that they may have strength*
*   to meet the days to come*
*   with steadfastness and patience;*
not sorrowing as those without hope,
*   but in thankful remembrance of your great goodness,*
*   and in the joyful expectation of eternal life*
*   with those they love.*
And this we ask in the Name of Jesus Christ our Savior.
Amen. (Anglican)

A prayer of confession and pardon:

Holy God, before you our hearts are open,
*   and from you no secrets are hidden.*
We bring to you now
*   our shame and sorrow for our sins.*
We have forgotten
*   that our life is from you and unto you.*

We have neither sought nor done your will.
We have not been truthful in our hearts,
  in our speech, in our lives.
We have not loved as we ought to love.
Help us and heal us,
  raising us from our sins into a better life,
  that we may end our days in peace,
  trusting in your kindness unto the end;
through Jesus Christ our Lord,
  who lives and reigns with you
  in the unity of the Holy Spirit,
  one God, now and for ever. Amen.

The prayer continues with the following:

Who is in a position to condemn?
Only Christ, Christ who died for us, who rose for us,
  who reigns at God's right hand and prays for us.
Thanks be to God who gives us the victory
  through our Lord Jesus Christ. (United Methodist)

For an untimely or tragic death, one or more of the following:

Jesus our Friend, you wept at the grave of Lazarus,
  you know all our sorrows.
Behold our tears, and bind up the wounds of our hearts.
Through the mystery of pain,
  bring us into closer communion with you
  and with one another.
Raise us from death into life.
And grant, in your mercy,
  that with Name of the deceased,
  who has passed within the veil,
  we may come to live, with you
  and with all whom we love, in our Father's home. Amen.
(Joseph Bernardin)

God of us all, we thank you for Christ's grace,
through which we pray to you in this dark hour.
A life we love has been torn from us.
Expectations the years once held have vanished.
The mystery of death has stricken us.
O God, you know the lives we live
and the deaths we die—
woven so strangely of purpose and of chance,
of reason and of the irrational,
of strength and of frailty, of happiness and of pain.
Into your hands we commend the soul
of Name of the deceased.
No mortal life you have made is without eternal meaning.
No earthly fate is beyond your redeeming.
Through your grace that can do far more
than we can think or imagine,
fulfill in Name of the deceased
your purpose that reaches beyond time and death.
Lead Name of the deceased *from strength to strength,*
and fit Name of the deceased
for love and service in your kingdom.
Into your hands also we commit our lives.
You alone, God, make us to dwell in safety.
Whom, finally, have we on earth or in heaven but you?
Help us to know the measure of our days,
and how frail we are.
Hold us in your keeping.
Forgive us our sins.
Save our minds from despair and our hearts from fear.
And guard and guide us with your peace. Amen.
(Thomas Miles)

Everliving God, in Christ's resurrection
you turned the disciples' despair into triumph,
their sorrow into joy.
Give us faith to believe
that every good that seems to be overcome by evil,

and every love that seems to be buried in death,
shall rise again to life eternal;
through Jesus Christ, who lives
and reigns with you for ever more.
Amen. (United Methodist)

At the service for a child, one or more of the following:

O God, whose dear Son took little children into his arms
and blessed them:
Give us grace, we pray,
to entrust this child
to your never-failing love and care;
and bring us all to your eternal life;
through the same Jesus Christ our Lord. Amen.
(United Methodist)

O God, we pray that you will keep in your tender love
the life of this child whom we hold in blessed memory.
Help us who continue here to serve you with constancy,
trusting in your promise of eternal life,
that hereafter we may be united
with your blessed children
in glory everlasting;
through Jesus Christ our Lord. Amen.
(United Methodist)

God our Father, your love gave us life,
and your care never fails.
Yours is the beauty of childhood,
and yours the light that shines in the face of age.
For all whom you have given to be dear to our hearts,
we thank you,
and especially for this child
you have taken to yourself.
Into the arms of your love we give his/her soul,
remembering Jesus' words,

"Let the children come unto me,
for of such is the kingdom of heaven."
To your love also we commend
the sorrowing parents and family.
Show compassion to them as a father to his children;
comfort them as a mother her little ones.
As their love follows their hearts' treasure,
help them to trust that love they once have known
is never lost,
that the child taken from their sight
lives forever in your presence.
Into your hands we also give ourselves,
our regret for whatever more
we might have been or done,
our need to trust you more and to pray,
all our struggles for a better life.
Comfort us all.
Keep tender and true the love
in which we hold one another.
Let not our longing for you ever cease.
May things unseen and eternal grow more real for us,
more full of meaning,
that in our living and dying you may be our peace.
Amen. (United Methodist)

O Lord, you keep little children in this present world,
and hold them close to yourself in the life to come.
Receive in peace the soul of your child
Name of the child,
for you have said, "Of such is my kingdom of
heaven." Amen. (United Methodist)

Almighty God, in your keeping
there is shelter from the storm,
and in your mercy
there is comfort for the sorrows of life.
Hear now our prayer

for those who mourn and are heavy laden.
Give to them strength to bear and do your will.
Lighten their darkness with your love.
Enable them to see
beyond the things of this mortal world
the promise of the eternal
Help them to know that your care
enfolds all your people,
that you are our refuge and strength,
and that underneath are your everlasting arms. Amen.
(United Methodist)

For a stillborn child, one or both of the following:

Almighty God, loving Parent of all your children,
we come in sorrow that Name of the child
has been taken from us so soon.
Sometimes the burdens of life almost overwhelm us.
Yet we put our full trust in you,
knowing that through your Son Jesus Christ
you are with us always.
We take comfort that your loving arms
surround us in our time of grief.
Be with Name of the child's mother,
who has carried him/her *with love for so long.*
We know you feel her disappointment and pain.
May her faith be renewed in the days ahead
as she regains her strength.
Be with Name of the child's father
and/or other family members.
You know the heaviness of his/their *heart(s).*
Pour out upon him/her *your gracious healing,*
in the name of Jesus Christ, the great Physician,
we pray. Amen. (United Methodist)

Blessed Jesus, lover of children,
in lowliness of heart we cry to you for help.

Expecting the life of a child,
  we have witnessed his/her death.
Our despair is profound,
  and we know you weep with us in our loss.
Help us to hear your consoling voice,
  and give healing to our grief, merciful Savior. Amen.
(United Methodist)

For a person who did not profess the Christian faith, pray one or more of the following:

O God our Father, Creator of us all,
  giver and preserver of all life:
We confess to you our slowness
  to accept death as part of your plan for life.
We confess our reluctance
  to commit to you those whom we love.
Restore our faith
  that we may come to trust in your care and providence;
  through Jesus Christ. Amen. (United Methodist, alt.)

O Lord, from everlasting to everlasting you are God.
Look down upon our sorrowing hearts today,
  we humbly pray,
  and be gracious to us.
Help all who mourn to cast every care upon you,
  and find comfort;
  through Jesus Christ. Amen. (United Methodist, alt.)

Almighty God, the fountain of all life,
  our refuge and strength and our help in trouble:
Enable us, we pray, to put our trust in you,
  that we may obtain comfort,
  and find grace to help in this and every time of need;
  through Jesus Christ. Amen. (United Methodist, alt.)

Eternal God, you know all things in earth and heaven.
So fill our hearts with trust in you
  that, by night and by day,
  at all times and in all seasons,
  we may without fear commit those who are dear to us
  to your never-failing love,
  for this life and the life to come. Amen.
(United Methodist)

✛ *Psalms*

The Psalms, revealing sorrow and joy, loss and hope, and grief and comfort, contain the best songs of the people of God. In many services of worship, the psalms follow the reading of the Old Testament lessons, as a response to the first or Old Testament reading. In funerals, there is no set order or sequence; thus a psalm or psalms may be read as the first Scripture or wherever they fit within the liturgy.

Psalm 23, ever since its inclusion in the very first 1549 English *Book of Common Prayer* in the service for the burial of the dead, is the most frequently used Scripture at funerals. The following is the King James Version of David's psalm. Other translations of Psalm 23 may also be sung or spoken:

Psalm 23

The Lord is my shepherd; I shall not want.
He maketh me to lie down in green pastures:
  he leadeth me beside the still waters.
He restoreth my soul:
  he leadeth me in the paths of righteousness
  for his name's sake.
Yea, though I walk
  through the valley of the shadow of death,
  I will fear no evil:
for thou art with me;
  thy rod and thy staff they comfort me.
Thou preparest a table before me
  in the presence of mine enemies:
thou anointest my head with oil;
  my cup runneth over.
Surely goodness and mercy shall follow me
  all the days of my life:
  and I will dwell in the house of the Lord for ever.

Many hymns are based on Psalm 23 and may be used with or in place of reading the psalm. These hymns include: "He Leadeth Me: O Blessed Thought," "The King of Love My Shepherd Is," and "The Lord's My Shepherd, I'll Want Not."

Psalm 130, a song of comfort and healing, may serve as a prayer of praise. This psalm can also serve as a prayer for illumination before the reading of other Scriptures.

Psalm 130

> *Out of the depths I cry unto thee, O Lord!*
> *Lord, hear my cry.*
> *Let thine ears be attentive*
> *to the voice of my supplication.*
> *If thou, Lord, should mark iniquities,*
> *Lord, who could stand?*
> *But there is forgiveness with thee,*
> *that thou may be feared.*
> *I wait for the Lord, my soul waits,*
> *and in God's word do I hope.*
> *My soul waits for the Lord*
> *more than those who watch for the morning.*
> *O Israel, hope in the Lord!*
> *For with the Lord is great mercy.*
> *With God is plenteous redemption,*
> *and the Lord will redeem Israel from all their sins.*
> *(KJV, alt.)*

Consider also:

Psalm 16	The Lord is my portion.
Psalm 27	Devotion and deliverance
Psalm 34	Thanksgiving for deliverance
Psalm 40	Thanksgiving for deliverance
Psalm 42	As a deer longs for flowing streams

Psalm 43	You are the God in whom I take refuge.
Psalm 46	God is our refuge and strength.
Psalm 71	Deliverance from evil
Psalm 77	Deliverance from trouble
Psalm 84	How lovely is your dwelling place.
Psalm 90	From everlasting to everlasting
Psalm 91	My God in whom I trust
Psalm 103	Bless the Lord, O my soul.
Psalm 106	God's love endures
Psalm 116	I will lift up the cup of salvation.
Psalm 118	Thanksgiving for deliverance
Psalm 121	I lift up my eyes to the hills.
Psalm 126	Prayer for deliverance
Psalm 139	O Lord, you have searched me.
Psalm 143	Prayer for deliverance
Psalm 145	The Lord is gracious and merciful.
Psalm 146	Praise the Lord, O my soul.

✛ *Old Testament Scriptures*

The specter of God's words, "You are dust, and to dust you shall return" (Genesis 3:19), hover over all the Scriptures. The people of God long to be set free from death, always knowing that in life and in death God is always with them.

One or more of the following Scriptures from the Hebrew Scriptures may be read by the pastor, family members, or friends of the deceased:

Isaiah 40:1-8 (alt.), God's promise of comfort:

> *Comfort, O comfort my people, says your God.*
> *Speak tenderly to Jerusalem, and cry to her*
> *   that she has served her term, that her penalty is paid,*
> *that she has received from the Lord's hand*
> *double for all her sins.*
> *A voice cries out:*
> *   "In the wilderness prepare the way of the Lord,*
> *   make straight in the desert a highway for our God.*
> *Every valley shall be lifted up,*
> *   and every mountain and hill be made low;*
> *the uneven ground shall become level,*
> *   and the rough places a plain.*
> *Then the glory of the Lord shall be revealed,*
> *   and all the people shall see it together,*
> *   for the mouth of the Lord has spoken."*
> *A voice says, "Cry out!"*
> *   And I said, "What shall I cry?"*
> *All people are grass,*
> *   their constancy is like the flower of the field.*
> *The grass withers, the flower fades,*
> *   when the breath of the Lord blows upon it;*
> *surely the people are grass.*
> *The grass withers, the flower fades;*
> *   but the word of our God will stand forever.*

Isaiah 40:28-31 (alt.), the prophet's promise for strength:

Have you not known? Have you not heard?
The Lord is an everlasting God,
  the Creator of the ends of the earth.
God does not faint or grow weary,
  the Lord's understanding is unsearchable.
God gives power to the faint,
  and strengthens the powerless.
Even youths will faint and be weary,
  and the young will fall exhausted;
but those who wait for the Lord
  shall renew their strength,
  they shall mount up with wings like eagles,
  they shall run and not be weary,
  they shall walk and not faint.

Exodus 14 (excerpts, alt.), a reading regarding our deliverance:

When the king of Egypt was told that the people of Israel had fled, the minds of Pharaoh and his officials were changed toward the people, and the Egyptians said, "What have we done, letting Israel leave our service?" So Pharaoh had his chariot made ready, and took his army with him; . . .

The Egyptians pursued the people of Israel, all Pharaoh's horses and chariots, his chariot drivers and his army; the Egyptians overtook the people of Israel camped by the sea. . . . As Pharaoh drew near, the Israelites looked back, and there were the Egyptians advancing on them. In great fear the Israelites cried out to the LORD.

The Israelites said to Moses, "Was it because there were no graves in Egypt that you have taken us away to die in the wilderness? What have you done to us, bringing us out of Egypt? Is this not the very thing we told you in

Egypt, 'Let us alone and let us serve the Egyptians'? For it would have been better for us to serve the Egyptians than to die in the wilderness."

But Moses said to the people, "Do not be afraid, stand firm, and see the deliverance that the LORD will accomplish for you today; for the Egyptians whom you see today you shall never see again. The LORD will fight for you, and you have only to keep still."...

The angel of God who was going before the Israelite army moved and went behind them; and the pillar of cloud moved from in front of the people of Israel and took its place behind them. The pillar of cloud came between the army of Egypt and the army of Israel. And so the cloud was there with the darkness, and the cloud lit up the night; one army did not come near the other army all night.

Then Moses stretched out his hand over the sea. The LORD drove the sea back by a strong east wind all night, and turned the sea into dry land; and the waters were divided. The Israelites went into the sea on dry ground, the waters forming a wall for them on their right and on their left.

The Egyptians pursued, and went into the sea after them, all of Pharaoh's horses, chariots, and chariot drivers. At the morning watch the LORD in the pillar of fire and cloud looked down upon the Egyptian army, and threw the Egyptian army into panic. The LORD clogged their chariot wheels so that they turned with difficulty. The Egyptians said, "Let us flee from the Israelites, for the LORD is fighting for them against Egypt."

Then the LORD said to Moses, "Stretch out your hand over the sea, so that the water may come back upon the

Egyptians, upon their chariots and chariot drivers." So Moses stretched out his hand over the sea, and at dawn the sea returned to its normal depth. As the Egyptians fled before it, the LORD tossed the Egyptians into the sea. The waters returned and covered the chariots and the chariot drivers...; not one of the Egyptians remained.

But the Israelites walked on dry ground through the sea, the waters forming a wall for them on their right and on their left. Thus the LORD saved Israel that day from the Egyptians;...Israel saw the great work that the LORD did against the Egyptians. So the people feared the LORD and believed in the LORD.

Isaiah 43–44 (excerpts, alt.), the prophet reminds us that God will deliver us:

But now says the LORD, God who created you, ...
  O Israel: Do not fear, for I, the LORD,
  have redeemed you;
  I have called you by name, you are mine.
When you pass through the waters, I will be with you;
  and through the rivers, they shall not overwhelm you;
when you walk through fire you shall not be burned,
  and the flame shall not consume you.
For I am the LORD your God,
  the Holy One of Israel, your Savior....
Do not fear, for I am with you;
I, the LORD your God,
  will bring your offspring from the east,
  and from the west I will gather you;
I will say to the north, "Give them up,"
  and to the south, "Do not withhold;
bring my sons from far away
  and my daughters from the end of the earth...
  everyone who is called by my name,

whom I created for my glory,
whom I formed and made."...
Do not remember the former things,
or consider the things of old.
I, the LORD, am about to do a new thing;
now it springs forth, do you not perceive it?
I will make a way in the wilderness
and rivers in the desert....
I am the LORD who blots out your transgressions
for my own sake,
and I will not remember your sins....
Thus says the LORD, the King of Israel,
and his Redeemer, the LORD of hosts:
I am the first and I am the last;
besides me there is no god....
Do not fear, or be afraid...
You are my witnesses!

Isaiah 55 (excerpts, alt.), a hymn of joy:

Ho, everyone who thirsts, come to the waters;
and you that have no money, come, buy and eat!
Come, buy wine and milk
without money and without price.
Why do you spend your money
for that which is not bread,
and your labor for that which does not satisfy?
Listen carefully to me, the LORD, and eat what is good,
and delight yourselves in rich food.
Incline your ear, and come to me;
listen, so that you may live.
I, the LORD, will make with you
an everlasting covenant, ...
Seek the LORD while God may be found,
call upon the LORD while God is near;
let the wicked forsake their way,
and the unrighteous their thoughts;

let them return to the LORD,
that God may have mercy on them. . . .
For my thoughts are not your thoughts,
nor are your ways my ways, says the LORD.
For as the heavens are higher than the earth,
so are my ways higher than your ways
and my thoughts than your thoughts. . . .
For you shall go out in joy, and be led back in peace;
the mountains and the hills before you
shall burst into song,
and all the trees of the field shall clap their hands.

Job 19:23-27, Job proclaims that his Redeemer lives:

O that my words were written down!
O that they were inscribed in a book!
O that with an iron pen and with lead
they were engraved on a rock forever!
For I know that my Redeemer lives,
and that at the last my Redeemer
will stand upon the earth;
and after my skin has been thus destroyed,
then in my flesh I shall see God,
whom I shall see on my side,
and my eyes shall behold, and not another.
My heart faints within me!

Proverbs 31 (excerpts), a celebration of a good woman:

A capable wife who can find?
She is far more precious than jewels.
The heart of her husband trusts in her.
She does him good, and not harm, all the days of her life.
She seeks wool and flax, and works with willing hands. . . .
Her hands hold the spindle.
She opens her hand to the poor, and reaches out her
hands to the needy. . . .

Her husband is known in the city gates,
    taking his seat among the elders of the land....
She opens her mouth with wisdom,
    and the teaching of kindness is on her tongue.
She looks well to the ways of her household,
    and does not eat the bread of idleness.
Her children rise up and call her happy;
    her husband too, and he praises her:
"Many women have done excellently,
    but you surpass them all."
Charm is deceitful, and beauty is vain,
    but a woman who fears the LORD is to be praised.
Give her a share in the fruit of her hands,
    and let her works praise her in the city gates.

Ecclesiastes 3:1-11 (excerpts), there is a time for everything:

For everything there is a season,
    and a time for every matter under heaven:
a time to be born, and a time to die;
    a time to plant, and a time to pluck up what is planted;
a time to kill, and a time to heal;
    a time to break down, and a time to build up;
a time to weep, and a time to laugh;
    a time to mourn, and a time to dance;
a time to throw away stones,
    and a time to gather stones together;
a time to embrace,
    and a time to refrain from embracing;
a time to seek, and a time to lose;
    a time to keep, and a time to throw away;
a time to tear, and a time to sew;
    a time to keep silence, and a time to speak;
a time to love, and a time to hate;
    a time for war, and a time for peace....
God has made everything suitable for its time.

Ezekiel 37 (excerpts, alt.), God promises the prophet Ezekiel that dry bones can live:

The hand of the LORD came upon me, Ezekiel, and God brought me out by the spirit of the LORD and set me down in the middle of a valley; the valley was full of bones. God led me all around the bones; there were very many bones lying in the valley, and they were very dry. God said to me, "Ezekiel, can these bones live?" I answered, "O Lord GOD, you know."

Then God said to me, "Prophesy to these bones, and say to them: O dry bones, hear the word of the LORD. Thus says the Lord GOD to these bones: I will cause breath to enter you, and you shall live. I will lay sinews on you, and will cause flesh to come upon you, and cover you with skin, and put breath in you, and you shall live; and you shall know that I am the LORD."

So I, Ezekiel, prophesied as I had been commanded; and as I prophesied, suddenly there was a noise, a rattling, and the bones came together, bone to its bone. I looked, and there were sinews on the bones, and flesh had come upon them, and skin had covered them; but there was no breath in them.

Then God said to me, "Prophesy to the breath, prophesy, Ezekiel, . . . Come from the four winds, O breath, and breathe upon these slain, that they may live." I prophesied as God commanded me, and the breath came into the bones, and they lived, and stood on their feet, a vast multitude.

Then God said to me, "Ezekiel, these bones are the whole house of Israel. They say, 'Our bones are dried up, and our hope is lost; we are cut off completely.'

Therefore prophesy, and say to the house of Israel. . . : I am going to open your graves, and bring you up from your graves, O my people; and I will bring you back to the land of Israel. And you shall know that I am the LORD, *when I open your graves, and bring you up from your graves, O my people."*

"I will put my spirit within you, and you shall live, and I will place you on your own soil; then you shall know that I, the LORD, *have spoken and will act," says the* LORD. . . . *My dwelling place shall be with them; and I will be their God, and they shall be my people."*

Consider also:

Genesis 15:15	Abraham's death
Genesis 22:1-18	Abraham and Isaac
Genesis 49:1, 29-33;	
50:1-2, 12-14	Jacob's death and Joseph's response
Exodus 15	Canticle of Moses and Miriam
Deuteronomy 33:27	God is your dwelling.
Joshua 3:14–4:7	Crossing over Jordan
2 Samuel 12:16-23	Death of David's child
Job 1:21	Job's faith
Job 14:1-12a	We are of few days.
Job 19:25-27	My Redeemer lives.
Isaiah 25:1, 6-9	God will swallow up death.
Isaiah 26:1-4, 19	Your dead shall live.
Isaiah 35:1-6, 10	Zion restored
Isaiah 41:8-10, 13	Do not fear.
Isaiah 57:14-19	Poem of consolation
Isaiah 61:1-4, 10-11	The Spirit of the Lord is upon me.
Isaiah 65:17-25	New heaven and new earth
Isaiah 66:10-13	As a mother comforts, so does God.

Lamentations 3:22-33   The Lord is good for those who wait.
Wisdom 3:1-5, 9   The righteous are in the hand of God.
Ezekiel 34:11-16   Shepherd of Israel
Micah 6:6-8   What does the Lord require?
Zephaniah 3:16-20   Restoration of Israel

✛ *Epistle and New Testament Scriptures*

The Epistles and every other New Testament writing originally addressed the first Christians between the time of Jesus Christ's resurrection and the anticipation of the coming of the Savior. Those persons knew persecution and death, yet through these Scriptures they remained faithful because of their hope in Christ's power over death.

One or more of the following Scriptures from the New Testament letters and writings may be read by the pastor, family members, or friends of the deceased:

1 Corinthians 15 (excerpts), Paul's proclamation of the good news:

Now I would remind you, brothers and sisters,
of the good news that I proclaimed to you,
> *which you in turn received, in which also you stand,*
> *through which also you are being saved.*
Now if Christ is proclaimed as raised from the dead,
> *how can some of you say*
> *there is no resurrection of the dead?*
For if the dead are not raised,
> *then Christ has not been raised.*
If Christ has not been raised,
> *your faith is futile and you are still in your sins.*
Then those also who have died in Christ have perished.
But in fact Christ has been raised from the dead,
> *the first fruits of those who have died. . . .*
What is sown is perishable,
> *what is raised is imperishable.*
It is sown in dishonor, it is raised in glory.
It is sown in weakness, it is raised in power.
It is sown a physical body, it is raised a spiritual body.
If there is a physical body, there is also a spiritual body.
When this perishable body puts on imperishability,
> *and this mortal body puts on immortality,*
then the saying that is written will be fulfilled:
"Death has been swallowed up in victory."

"Where, O death, is your victory?
   Where, O death, is your sting?"
But thanks be to God,
   who gives us the victory through our Lord Jesus Christ.

Revelation 21 (excerpts, alt.), the prophet John envisions a new heaven and earth:

Then I saw a new heaven and a new earth;
   for the first heaven and the first earth
   had passed away,
   and the sea was no more.
And I saw the holy city, the new Jerusalem,
   coming down out of heaven from God,
   prepared as a bride adorned for her husband.
And I heard a loud voice from the throne saying,
   "See, the home of God is among mortals.
The Lord will dwell with them as their God;
   they will be God's peoples,
   and God himself will be with them;
   God will wipe every tear from their eyes.
Death will be no more;
   mourning and crying and pain will be no more,
   for the first things have passed away."
And the one who was seated on the throne, Jesus Christ,
   said, "See, I am making all things new."
Also the Christ said,
"Write this, for these words
   are trustworthy and true." . . .
"It is done! I am the Alpha and the Omega,
   the beginning and the end.
To the thirsty I will give water
   as a gift from the spring of the water of life.
Those who conquer will inherit these things,
   and I will be their God and they will be my children."

Romans 8 (excerpts, alt.), Paul's promise of the love of God:

There is therefore now no condemnation
for those who are in Christ Jesus.
For the law of the Spirit of life in Christ Jesus
has set you free from the law of sin and of death.
If the Spirit of God
who raised Jesus from the dead dwells in you,
God who raised Christ from the dead
will give life to your mortal bodies also
through God's Spirit that dwells in you.
For all who are led by the Spirit of God
are children of God,
and if children, then heirs,
heirs of God and joint heirs with Christ—
if, in fact, we suffer with Christ
so that we may also be glorified with Christ.
I consider that the sufferings of this present time
are not worth comparing with the glory
about to be revealed to us.
We know that all things work together for good
for those who love God,
who are called according to God's purpose.
What then are we to say about these things?
If God is for us, who is against us?
God who did not withhold his own Son,
but gave Christ up for all of us,
will God not with Christ also give us everything else?
Who will separate us from the love of Christ?
Will hardship, or distress, or persecution,
or famine, or nakedness, or peril, or sword?
No!
In all these things we are more than conquerors
through Christ who loved us.
For I am convinced that neither death, nor life,
nor angels, nor rulers, nor things present,
nor things to come,

nor powers, nor height, nor depth,
nor anything else in all creation,
will be able to separate us from the love of God
in Christ Jesus our Lord.

2 Corinthians 4 (excerpts), Paul calls the Corinthians and us to give glory to God:

For we do not proclaim ourselves;
we proclaim Jesus Christ as Lord
and ourselves as your slaves for Jesus' sake.
For it is the God who said,
"Let light shine out of darkness,"
who has shown in our hearts...
We are afflicted in every way, but not crushed;
perplexed, but not driven to despair;
persecuted, but not forsaken;
struck down, but not destroyed;
always carrying in the body the death of Jesus,
so that the life of Jesus
may also be made visible in our bodies.
For while we live, we are always being given up to death
for Jesus' sake,
so that the life of Jesus
may be made visible in our mortal flesh.
Because we know that God who raised the Lord Jesus
will raise us also with Jesus,
and will bring us with you into God's presence.
So we do not lose heart.
[Even though our outer nature is wasting away,
our inner nature is being renewed day by day.
For this slight momentary affliction
is preparing us for an eternal weight of glory
beyond all measure,
because we look not at what can be seen
but at what cannot be seen;

for what can be seen is temporary,
but what cannot be seen is eternal.]

Ephesians 1 and 2 (excerpts, alt.), Paul reminds Christians that we are
all alive in Christ:

I, Paul, have heard of your faith in the Lord Jesus
and your love toward all the saints,
and for this reason I do not cease to give thanks for you
as I remember you in my prayers.
I pray that the God of our Lord Jesus Christ,
the Father of glory,
may give you a spirit of wisdom and revelation
as you come to know Christ,
so that, with the eyes of your heart enlightened,
you may know what is the hope
to which Christ has called you,
what are the riches of Christ's glorious inheritance
among the saints.
God put this power to work in Christ
when God raised Christ from the dead
and seated Christ at God's right hand
in the heavenly places,
far above all rule and authority
and power and dominion,
and above every name that is named,
not only in this age but also in the age to come.
And God has put all things under Christ's feet
and has made Christ the head
over all things for the church.
All of us once lived among them
in the passions of our flesh,
following the desires of flesh and senses,
and we were by nature children of wrath,
like everyone else.
But God, who is rich in mercy,

87

out of the great love with which God loved us
even when we were dead through our trespasses,
made us alive together with Christ—
by grace you have been saved—
and raised us up with Christ
and seated us with Christ
in the heavenly places in Christ Jesus,
so that in the ages to come
God might show the immeasurable riches
of God's grace . . . in Christ Jesus.

1 Peter 1 (excerpts, alt.), Peter proclaims that we are blessed by God:

Blessed be the God and Father of our Lord Jesus Christ!
By God's great mercy
God has given us a new birth into a living hope
through the resurrection of Jesus Christ from the dead,
and into an inheritance
that is imperishable, undefiled, and unfading,
kept in heaven for you.
In this you rejoice,
even if now for a little while
you have had to suffer various trials,
so that the genuineness of your faith—
being more precious than gold that,
though perishable, is tested by fire
—may be found to result in praise
and glory and honor
when Jesus Christ is revealed.
Although you have not seen Jesus Christ, you love him;
and even though you do not see Jesus Christ now,
you believe in Christ
and rejoice with an indescribable and glorious joy.
Therefore prepare your minds for action;
discipline yourselves;
set all your hope on the grace

that Jesus Christ will bring you when he is revealed.
Jesus Christ was destined
before the foundation of the world,
but was revealed at the end of the ages for your sake.
Through Jesus Christ you have come to trust in God,
who raised Christ from the dead and gave him glory,
so that your faith and hope are set on God.
You have been born anew,
not of perishable but of imperishable seed,
through the living and enduring word of God.
For "All flesh is like grass
and all its glory like the flower of grass.
The grass withers, and the flower falls,
but the word of the Lord endures forever."

Revelation 7 (excerpts, alt.), John's vision of the multitude of the redeemed:

I, John, saw another angel
ascending from the rising of the sun,
having the seal of the living God,
and the angel called with a loud voice saying,
"Do not damage the earth or the sea or the trees,
until we have marked the servants of our God
with a seal on their foreheads."
And I heard the number of those who were sealed,
sealed out of every tribe of the people of Israel:
After this I looked, and there was a great multitude
that no one could count,
from every nation,
from all tribes and peoples and languages,
standing before the throne and before the Lamb,
robed in white, with palm branches in their hands.
The multitude cried out in a loud voice, saying,
"Salvation belongs to our God
who is seated on the throne,

and to the Lamb!"
And all the angels stood around the throne
  and around the elders and the four living creatures,
and the angels fell on their faces before the throne
  and worshiped God, singing,
  "Amen! Blessing and glory and wisdom
  and thanksgiving
  and honor and power and might
  be to our God forever and ever! Amen."
Then one of the elders addressed me, saying,
  "These are they
  who have come out of the great ordeal;
  they have washed their robes
  and made them white in the blood of the Lamb.
For this reason they are before the throne of God,
  and worship God day and night within God's temple,
  and the Lamb who is seated on the throne
  will shelter them.
They will hunger no more, and thirst no more;
  the sun will not strike them, nor any scorching heat;
for the Lamb at the center of the throne
  will be their shepherd,
  and the Lamb will guide them
  to springs of the water of life,
  and God will wipe away every tear from their eyes."

Consider also:

Acts 10:34-43	Peter's sermon on Jesus' resurrection
Romans 5:1-11, 17-21	Peace with God through faith
Romans 6:3-11	Dying and rising with Christ
Romans 14:7-9	Christ, Lord of the dead and the living
2 Corinthians 5:1-11a, 14-20	Away from the body, at home in the Lord

Ephesians 3:14-21	Bow before God; know the love of Christ.
Philippians 3:7-21	The power of Christ's resurrection
Colossians 3:1-17	Raised with Christ
1 Thessalonians 4:13–5:11	Concerning those who sleep
2 Timothy 4:6-8, 17-18	I have fought the good fight.
Hebrews 11–12	The saints of God
1 John 3:1-3	We shall be like God.
Revelation 14:1-3, 6-7, 12-13	Blessed are the dead in the Lord.

✛ *Gospel Scriptures*

The essential good news of Matthew, Mark, Luke, and John is the promise of resurrection beyond death of Jesus Christ. In the life, teachings, and miracles of Jesus Christ, the first followers discovered power over demonic forces and ultimately death.

The congregation may be invited to stand for the reading of the Gospel, or for another of the other Scriptures.

One or more of the following Scriptures from the Gospels may be read by the pastor, family members, or friends of the deceased.

John 14 (excerpts), the Gospel of John proclaims the peace of God:

[Jesus said,] "Do not let your hearts be troubled.
Believe in God, believe also in me.
In my Father's house there are many dwelling places.
If it were not so,
   would I have told you
   that I go to prepare a place for you?
And if I go and prepare a place for you,
   I will come again and will take you to myself,
   so that where I am, there you may be also.
And you know the way to the place where I am going.
I will not leave you orphaned;
   I am coming to you.
In a little while the world will no longer see me,
   but you will see me;
   because I live, you also will live.
I have said these things to you
   while I am still with you. . . .
Peace I leave with you; my peace I give to you.
I do not give to you as the world gives.
Do not let your hearts be troubled,
and do not let them be afraid."

Luke 23:33-43 (excerpts), Jesus shares paradise for the thief on the cross:

*When Jesus and the soldiers came to the place
that is called The Skull,
the Romans crucified Jesus there with the criminals,
one criminal on Jesus' right
and one criminal on Jesus' left.
One of the criminals who were hanged there
kept deriding Jesus
and saying, "Are you not the Messiah?
Save yourself and us!"
But the other criminal rebuked the first, saying,
"Do you not fear God,
since you are under the same sentence
of condemnation?
And we indeed have been condemned justly,
for we are getting what we deserve for our deeds,
but this man Jesus has done nothing wrong."
Then the criminal said,
"Jesus, remember me
when you come into your kingdom."
Jesus replied, "Truly I tell you,
today you will be with me in Paradise."*

Luke 24 (excerpts, alt.), Jesus appears to his two disciples at Emmaus:

*Now on that same day of Easter, two of Jesus' followers
were going to a village called Emmaus, about seven
miles from Jerusalem, and talking with each other about
all these things that had happened. While the two followers were talking and discussing, Jesus himself came
near and went with the followers, but their eyes were
kept from recognizing Jesus.*

*And Jesus said to the two, "What are you discussing
with each other while you walk along?"*

*The two stood still, looking sad. Then one of them,
whose name was Cleopas, answered Jesus,*

"Are you the only stranger in Jerusalem who does not know the things that have taken place there in these days?" Jesus asked them, "What things?"

The two replied, "The things about Jesus of Nazareth, who was a prophet mighty in deed and word before God and all the people, and how our chief priests and leaders handed Jesus over to be condemned to death and crucified him. But we had hoped that Jesus was the one to redeem Israel. Yes, and besides all this, it is now the third day since these things took place. Moreover, some women of our group astounded us. The women were at the tomb early this morning, and when they did not find Jesus' body there, the women came back and told us that they had indeed seen a vision of angels who said that Jesus was alive. Some of those who were with us went to the tomb and found it just as the women had said; but they did not see Jesus."

Then Jesus said to them, "Oh, how foolish you are, and how slow of heart to believe all that the prophets have declared! Was it not necessary that the Messiah should suffer these things and then enter into his glory?" Then beginning with Moses and all the prophets, Jesus interpreted to them the things about himself in all the scriptures.

As they came near the village to which they were going, Jesus walked ahead as if he were going on. But the two followers urged Jesus strongly, saying, "Stay with us, because it is almost evening and the day is now nearly over." So Jesus went in to stay with them.

When Jesus was at the table with them, Jesus took bread, blessed and broke the bread, and gave it to them. Then their eyes were opened, and they recognized Jesus; and he vanished from their sight.

The two followers said to each other, "Were not our hearts burning within us while Jesus was talking to us on the road, while he was opening the scriptures to us?"

That same hour they got up and returned to Jerusalem; and they found the eleven disciples and their companions gathered together. The eleven were saying, "The Lord has risen indeed, and Jesus has appeared to Simon!" Then the two followers told what had happened on the road, and how Jesus had been made known to them in the breaking of the bread.

John 11 (excerpts, alt.), the raising of Lazarus

Now a certain man was ill, Lazarus of Bethany, the village of Mary and her sister Martha. Mary was the one who anointed the Lord with perfume and wiped his feet with her hair; Mary's brother Lazarus was ill.

So the sisters sent a message to Jesus, "Lord, Lazarus whom you love is ill." But when Jesus heard it, he said, "This illness does not lead to death; rather it is for God's glory, so that the Son of God may be glorified through it." Accordingly, though Jesus loved Martha and her sister Mary and Lazarus, after having heard that Lazarus was ill, Jesus stayed two days longer in the place where he was. Then after this Jesus said to the disciples, "Let us go to Judea again."

The disciples said to Jesus, "Rabbi, the Jews were just now trying to stone you, and are you going there again?" Jesus told them, "Our friend Lazarus has fallen asleep, but I am going there to awaken him." The disciples said to Jesus, "Lord, if Lazarus has fallen asleep, he will be all right." Jesus, however, had been speaking about Lazarus' death, but they thought that Jesus was referring merely to sleep.

Then Jesus told the disciples plainly, "Lazarus is dead. For your sake I am glad I was not there, so that you may believe. But let us go to Lazarus."

When Jesus arrived, he found that Lazarus had already been in the tomb four days. Many of the Jews had come to Martha and Mary to console them about their brother. When Martha heard that Jesus was coming, Martha went and met him, while Mary stayed at home. Martha said to Jesus, "Lord, if you had been here, my brother would not have died. But even now I know that God will give you whatever you ask of God."

Jesus said to Martha, "Your brother will rise again." Martha said to Jesus, "I know that Lazarus will rise again in the resurrection on the last day."

Jesus said to her, "I am the resurrection and the life. Those who believe in me, even though they die, will live, and everyone who lives and believes in me will never die. Do you believe this?" Martha said to Jesus, "Yes, Lord, I believe that you are the Messiah, the Son of God, the one coming into the world."

When Mary came where Jesus was and saw him, Mary knelt at Jesus' feet and said to him, "Lord, if you had been here, my brother would not have died."

When Jesus saw Mary weeping, and the Jews who came with her also weeping, he was greatly disturbed in spirit and deeply moved. Jesus said, "Where have you laid Lazarus?" They said to him, "Lord, come and see." Jesus began to weep.

So the Jews said, "See how Jesus loved Lazarus!"

Then Jesus, again greatly disturbed, came to the tomb.

It was a cave, and a stone was lying against it. Jesus said, "Take away the stone."

Martha, the sister of the dead man, said to Jesus, "Lord, already there is a stench because Lazarus has been dead four days." Jesus said to Martha, "Did I not tell you that if you believed, you would see the glory of God?"

So they took away the stone. And Jesus looked upward and said, "Father, I thank you for having heard me. I knew that you always hear me, but I have said this for the sake of the crowd standing here, so that they may believe that you sent me." When Jesus had said this, he cried with a loud voice, "Lazarus, come out!"

The dead man came out, Lazarus' hands and feet bound with strips of cloth, and his face wrapped in a cloth. Jesus said to them, "Unbind Lazarus, and let him go."

Many of the Jews therefore, who had come with Mary and had seen what Jesus did, believed in Jesus.

Matthew 11:25-30 (excerpts), Jesus invites all who labor to come to him:

Jesus said,
  "All things have been handed over to me
    by my Father;
  Come to me, all you that are weary
  and are carrying heavy burdens,
    and I will give you rest.
  Take my yoke upon you, and learn from me;
  for I am gentle and humble in heart,
    and you will find rest for your souls.
  For my yoke is easy, and my burden is light."

Consider also:

Matthew 5:1-12	The Beatitudes
Matthew 6:19-21	Do not lay up treasures on earth.
Matthew 25:31-46	As you did it to one of the least
Matthew 28:1-10, 16-20	Jesus' resurrection: Go make disciples.
Mark 16:1-8	The open tomb: Jesus goes before you.
Luke 1:67-75	Canticle of Zechariah
Luke 12:22-40	Do not be anxious; be ready.
Luke 24:1-12	The empty tomb
John 3:13-17	God's gift of eternal life
John 5:19-29	Whoever hears and believes has life.
John 6:30-40, 47-51	Jesus, the bread of life
John 10:1-18, 27-30	Jesus, the Good Shepherd
John 12:20-36	Unless a grain of wheat dies
John 15:1-17	The vine and the branches
John 16:12-22, 33	Sorrow becomes joy.
John 20	Jesus' resurrection

✛ *Additional Scriptures for Unique Services*

Scriptures for a stillborn child:

Psalm 23 (page 70)	The Lord is my shepherd.
Psalm 130 (page 71)	Out of the depths I cry to you.
2 Corinthians 1:3-7	God consoles us in all our affliction.
Matthew 11:28-30 (page 97)	Come to me, all who carry heavy burdens.

Scriptures at the death of a child:

1 Samuel 1:28	The dedication of a child
2 Samuel 12:16-23	David and the death of his child
Isaiah 65:17-25	An infant who lives but a few days
Lamentations 3:19-26, 31-33	Remember my affliction; God is good
Joel 2:1, 12-13, 23-25a, 26-29	Your sons and daughters will see visions.
Psalm 103:6-18	As a father pities his children
Matthew 11:25-30	God revealed to infants
Matthew 18:1-5, 10-14	Children are greatest in God's kingdom.
Matthew 19:13-15	Let the children come to me.
Mark 5:35-43	Jesus' raising of the ruler's daughter

Scriptures for a young person:

Job 1:21	Job mourns his children.
Ecclesiastes 12:1	A youth's religion
Luke 7:14	Jesus raises a young man.

99

1 John 2:14   The strength of youth

Scriptures for an older adult:

Genesis 15:15   Peace at the end of many years
Psalm 91:16   The glory of a long life
2 Timothy 4:7-8   Keep the faith

Scriptures for a Christian mother:

Proverbs 31 (page 78)   A godly woman
Isaiah 66:13   Comfort by a mother
2 Timothy 1:5   A godly mother

Scriptures for a Christian father:

Genesis 18:19   A father's teaching
1 Kings 2:2-3   A father's charge

Scriptures for an untimely or tragic death:

Lamentations 3:19-26, 31-33   Bless the Lord, who redeems
                                       from death.

Revelation 21:1-6;
  22:1-5 (see page 84)   God will wipe away every tear.
Mark 4:35-41   Jesus' calming of the storm
Luke 15:11-32   The prodigal son
John 6:35-40   God's will that nothing be lost

Scriptures for a person who did not profess the Christian faith:

Ecclesiastes 3:1-11 (page 79)   For everything there is a season.
Lamentations 3:1-9, 19-26   God's steadfast love
Psalm 39   Make me to know the measure
                                       of my days.

Romans 14:7-13	Why do you pass judgment?
Matthew 5:1-12	The Beatitudes
Matthew 25:31-46	As you did it to one of the least
Luke 20:27-39	God of the living, to whom all live

✛ *Sermons, Homilies, and Eulogies*

A sermon may be preached, proclaiming the gospel in the face of death. The sermon, the living Word from God for the people of God, may lead into, or include, the following acts of Naming and Witness (page 104).

Homily (a short sermon) or Eulogy (a statement of tribute or affirmation) are other names for this central act of worship.

This proclamation of the Word should be brief; this is not the time for oratorical extravagance.

The sermon should be focused: a brief moment of exegesis; the highlights of a person's life, not every detail; the naming of those who most mourn, not every name of every family member and friend.

Remember that there are several audiences listening to the sermon: the grieving family, the congregation of believers, and family and friends of the deceased who may not be Christian. Regarding the family, do look directly at the family often during the service.

Regarding those who are not Christian, the sermon is not the best time to invite persons to commit themselves to Jesus Christ in a public way. A more compelling proclamation of the good news invites persons who do not follow Jesus Christ to understand the faith that the deceased possessed. There are other and better times to speak about public conversion.

If the pastor feels a need to invite persons to come to the Communion Table or Altar to kneel and pray, make the invitation as broad as possible. Instead of only inviting persons to make a first commitment to follow Jesus, invite persons to come and pray for themselves, for the family, for all who mourn, and for themselves.

The sermon, therefore, has several foci:

1. The mystery, power, and promise of Christ's death and resurrection. Pick one key text and stay with it.
2. The life of the deceased in honest yet affirmative ways. Tell what was best about the departed.
3. Comfort for the family and friends. Praise them for their faithfulness and give them hope for tomorrow.

One useful pastoral offering is to present to the family a copy of the sermon following the service. The text may be written out fully or simply the outline provided to each member of the family. The gift could also include a copy of all the Scriptures and prayers used in the service. Such a gift will be a honored possession and provide a touchstone for future remembrances and comfort during grief.

✠ *Naming and Witness*

This act of worship invites the gathered congregation to celebrate briefly the deceased and offer support for the family. Pastor, family, friends, and members of the congregation may briefly voice their thankfulness to God for the grace they have received in the life of the deceased and their Christian faith and joy. Naming and Witness often involves a time of tears and laughter.

The life and death of the deceased may be gathered up in the reading of a memorial or appropriate statement written by a family member or friends, read either by the pastor or others. At the funeral of my greatgrandfather and grandmother, my mother wrote a collection of her thoughts, which were read by the pastor.

Some families have the time and ability to create a multi-media DVD or PowerPoint presentation, with or without music, about the life of the deceased. Such a showing could also take place during the Family Hour or Wake before the service or at a reception before or following the funeral or memorial service.

Some traditions include the reading of the obituary of the deceased during this time. Often times, however, this tradition detracts from the service as persons hear or read what they already know. The obituary may be printed in full in a worship bulletin.

A poem or other reading may be presented. Songs may be sung. An interpretative dance may be shared. Other signs of faith, hope, and love may be exchanged, such as a gift or memorial to the family.

At the death of a person with political position or celebrity status, the time of Naming and Witness may involve many persons who wish to reflect on different aspects of the deceased's life. In such a case, the pastor or family may wish to assign different topics to different speakers.

Acts of worship during this time may also include the passing of the peace (greeting one another in the name of God), placing flowers on the casket, reading from the deceased's favorite book or favorite Scripture, showing a few favorite pictures, displaying symbols of the deceased's occupation or roles in the church, and even recognizing particular persons who have traveled a great distance or endured a hardship to attend the funeral (their presence itself is a witness).

One pattern comes from the Quaker tradition. Following a time of silence, everyone sits. Then, anyone who feels moved by the Holy Spirit may stand and speak. Persons may quietly recall a memory, share a prayer, or read a poem or Scripture to recall the strengths of the deceased and the gifts received from the departed. The congregation uses its collective wisdom to channel the presence of God to minister to one another.

Such a time of Naming and Witness has risks. Persons may share inappropriate memories. Some folk may wish to air or resolve old grievances. Many persons are fearful of speaking aloud and do not speak well in public. Voices tremble and tears will interrupt. Some persons simply do not know when to stop speaking. Good pastors learn to anticipate such actions and know how to gently regain control. For example, the pastor may stand beside those speaking and with a nod or touch give encouragement to continue or indicate that time is up. Sometimes, the pastor may need to respond to an emotional or angry or uncharitable witness with a word of grace. Stay calm but in control.

Yet, the risks of Naming and Witness are worth taking. When the Holy Spirit is present, some of the most unexpected and beautiful stories are told as persons say goodbye to a family member or friend. Oratorical polish may be superseded by heart-felt stories of love. When congregations gather to embody love and support, God is present. With tears, holy silences, and laughter, healing begins.

To assist with this time, in the pastoral visits before the funeral, the pastor should discuss the possibility of family members or friends to speak. Would a child or grandchild like to speak, either for themselves or for the family? Would the spouse of the deceased like to offer thanks for all the words and actions of kindness that have been received? Is a close friend able to collect the memories of colleagues and neighbors? Would the family welcome opening the service to others speaking besides the pastor?

Other occasions to remember the deceased are plentiful, and should not be limited to the funeral itself. On the anniversary of a death, All Saints Day or Sunday, a Homecoming, or a cemetery Decoration

Sunday may also be opportunities to remember the deceased by name and with memories. See pages 138-42 for prayers that may be used on any of these occasions.

"If Death My Friend and Me Divide" by Charles Wesley is one of many hymns and poems that might be read during this time (United Methodist Hymnal # 656).

If death my friend and me divide,
    thou dost not, Lord, my sorrow chide,
or frown my tears to see;
    restrained from passionate excess,
thou bidst me mourn in calm distress
    for them that rest in thee.

I feel a strong immortal hope,
    which bears my mournful spirit up
beneath its mountain load;
    redeemed from death, and grief, and pain,
I soon shall find my friend again
    within the arms of God.

Pass a few fleeting moments more
    and death the blessing shall restore
which death has snatched away;
    for me thou wilt the summons send,
and give me back my parted friend
    in that eternal day.

✠ *Creeds and Affirmations of Faith*

A creed, a historic statement of orthodox faith, or affirmation of faith is one way for the whole congregation to participate in the service. As a response to the Scriptures and sermon, a creed or affirmation of faith becomes a new offering of the faith of the congregation. Because persons come from many different traditions, when a creed is used, print the text in the worship bulletin. Typically, a congregation stands for the creed.

A hymn or musical response may either follow or precede the creed or affirmation of faith.

The Apostles' Creed, Traditional Version, has been used by Protestants, Orthodox, and Roman Catholics as an essential statement of classic Christianity since the third century. Often used at baptisms, the Apostles' Creed at a funeral reminds persons of their communion with God in life and death:

> *I believe in God the Father Almighty,*
> *   maker of heaven and earth;*
> *And in Jesus Christ his only Son our Lord:*
> *   who was conceived by the Holy Spirit,*
> *   born of the Virgin Mary,*
> *   suffered under Pontius Pilate,*
> *   was crucified, dead, and buried;*
> *the third day he arose from the dead;*
> *he ascended into heaven,*
> *   and sitteth at the right hand*
> *   of God the Father Almighty;*
> *from thence he shall come to judge*
> *   the quick and the dead.*
> *I believe in the Holy Spirit,*
> *   the holy catholic church,*
> *   the communion of saints,*
> *   the forgiveness of sins,*
> *   the resurrection of the body,*
> *   and the life everlasting. Amen.*

The Apostles' Creed, Ecumenical Version, is a 1987, ecumenically accepted modern English translation:

I believe in God, the Father Almighty,
  creator of heaven and earth.
I believe in Jesus Christ, his only Son, our Lord,
  who was conceived by the Holy Spirit,
  born of the Virgin Mary,
  suffered under Pontius Pilate,
  was crucified, died, and was buried;
  he descended to the dead.
  On the third day he rose again;
  he ascended into heaven,
  is seated at the right hand of the Father,
  and will come again to judge the living and the dead.
I believe in the Holy Spirit,
  the holy catholic church,
  the communion of saints,
  the forgiveness of sins,
  the resurrection of the body,
  and the life everlasting. Amen.

A Statement of Faith of the United Church of Canada is a more recent affirmation, whose final phrases are an exceptionally strong profession of faith:

We are not alone, we live in God's world.
We believe in God:
  who has created and is creating,
  who has come in Jesus, the Word made flesh,
  to reconcile and make new,
  who works in us and others by the Spirit.
We trust in God.
We are called to be the church:
  to celebrate God's presence,
  to love and serve others,

to seek justice and resist evil,
to proclaim Jesus, crucified and risen,
our judge and our hope.
In life, in death, in life beyond death,
God is with us.
We are not alone.
Thanks be to God. Amen.

An Affirmation from Romans 8:35-38 (excerpts, alt.), while not a creed, is ideal for funerals and times of distress:

Who will separate us from the love of Christ?
Will hardship, or distress,
or persecution, or famine,
or nakedness, or peril, or sword?
No!
In all these things we are more than conquerors
through Jesus Christ who loved us.
We are convinced that neither
death, nor life,
nor angels, nor rulers,
nor things present, nor things to come,
nor powers, nor height, nor depth,
nor anything else in all creation,
will be able to separate us from the love of God
in Christ Jesus our Lord.
Thanks be to God! Amen.

An Affirmation from 1 Corinthians 15:1-6 and Colossians 1:15-20, focuses on the saving grace of Jesus Christ:

This is the good news which we have received,
in which we stand, and by which we are saved:
Christ died for our sins,
was buried, was raised on the third day,
and appeared first to the women,

then to Peter and the twelve,
and then to many faithful witnesses.
We believe Jesus is the Christ,
the Anointed One of God,
the firstborn of all creation,
the firstborn from the dead,
in whom all things hold together,
in whom the fullness of God
was pleased to dwell
by the power of the Spirit.
Christ is the head of the body, the church,
and by the blood of the cross
reconciles all things to God. Amen.
(United Methodist)

A modern Canticle of Hope (Rev. 21;1-6; 23-24; 22:5, 12, 20):

We shall see a new heaven and earth,
for the old will pass away.
We shall see a new Jerusalem,
the holy city descending from heaven.
The city shall need no sun or moon,
for God's glory will be its light,
for God's Lamb will be its lamp,
and by its light the nations shall walk.
We shall hear a loud voice from the throne:
"Behold, God's dwelling is with mortals.
Indeed, God will dwell with them
and they will be God's people."
God shall wipe away all our tears,
and there shall be no more death.
Mourning, crying, and pain shall cease,
for all former things will pass away.
We shall hear One speak from the throne:
"Behold, I make all things new.
I am Alpha and Omega,

the beginning and the end."
Our Lord testifies to these things:
"Behold, I am coming soon."
The grace of the Lord is with us.
Amen. Come, Lord Jesus! Come!

✠ *Prayer of Great Thanksgiving for Holy Communion*

Holy Communion is first and foremost a feast of resurrection. As two of the first disciples saw Jesus in the village of Emmaus on the day of Easter in the breaking of the bread (Luke 24:13-35, see page 93), increasingly, Holy Communion is a part of funerals. In a tradition that goes back at least to the third century after Christ, such as in the Roman catacombs, the service unites the congregation with the saints in all times and places. As a congregation shares the bread and cup, so they are in communion with Christ, one another, and all the saints. The meal becomes a foretaste of the heavenly banquet.

The pastor, by tradition and ordination, presides at the Lord's Table, standing behind the table and offering the prayer facing the people. Yet other topics need to be planned.

Who will serve the congregation the bread and cup? It may be an important witness for members of the family or close friends to help serve the meal.

Who will receive? Usually, the family of the deceased will receive first, followed by the congregation. Because funerals often include people from many religious traditions, there should be no pressure that would embarrass those who for whatever reason do not choose to receive Holy Communion. Before the elements are distributed, the pastor should offer a clear invitation to the congregation. Such an invitation (which might also be printed in the worship bulletin for persons to read before the service) might be:

> *Christ invites to his Table all who have been baptized and are members of Christ's universal church. We also understand if you do not wish to participate in the Holy Meal.*

Or the following may be said:

*We invite to the Lord's Table all who wish to commune
with Christ and this family, as a foretaste of the heavenly
banquet.*

Each tradition has its own Eucharistic prayers. The following Prayer of
Great Thanksgiving is United Methodist, alt.:

The Lord be with you.
And also with you.
Lift up your hearts.
We lift them up to the Lord.
Let us give thanks to the Lord our God.
It is right to give our thanks and praise.

The pastor may raise hands.

It is right,
    that we should always and everywhere,
    and especially in times of life and death,
    give thanks to you, Almighty God,
    who breathed into us the breath of life.

And so, with your people on earth
    and all the company of heaven
    we praise your name and join their unending hymn:

**Holy, holy, holy Lord, God of power and might,
heaven and earth are full of your glory.
Hosanna in the highest!
Blessed is he who comes in the name of the Lord.
Hosanna in the highest!**

*Holy are you, and blessed is your Son Jesus Christ.
By the baptism of his suffering, death, and resurrection
    you gave birth to your Church,
    delivered us from slavery to sin and death,
    and made with us a new covenant*

CHRISTIAN FUNERALS

by water and the Spirit.
When the Lord Jesus ascended,
   he promised to be with us always
   in the power of your Word and Holy Spirit.

The pastor may hold hands, palms down, over the bread, or touch the bread, or lift the bread.

On the night in which he gave himself up for us,
   Jesus took bread,
   gave thanks to you, broke the bread,
   gave it to his disciples, and said:
"Take, eat; this is my body which is given for you.
Do this in remembrance of me."
When the supper was over Jesus took the cup,
   gave thanks to you, gave it to his disciples, and said
"Drink from this, all of you;
   this is my blood of the new covenant,
   poured out for you and for many
   for the forgiveness of sins.
Do this, as often as you drink it, in remembrance of me."

And so, in remembrance
   of these your mighty acts in Jesus Christ,
we offer ourselves in praise and thanksgiving
   as a holy and living sacrifice,
   in union with Christ's offering for us,
as we proclaim the mystery of faith:

Christ has died; Christ is risen; Christ will come again.

Pour out your Holy Spirit on us, gathered here,
   and on these gifts of bread and wine.
Make them be for us the body and blood of Christ,
   that we may be for the world the body of Christ,
   redeemed by his blood.

The pastor may raise hands.

> *By your Spirit make us one with Christ,*
>   *one with each other,*
>   *and one in communion with all your saints,*
>   *especially* Name of the deceased
>   *and all those most dear to us,*
>   *whom we now remember in the silence of our hearts.*

Observe a brief time of silence for remembrance.

> *Finally, by your grace, bring them and all of us to that table*
>   *where your saints feast for ever in your heavenly home.*
> *Through your Son Jesus Christ,*
>   *with the Holy Spirit in your holy Church,*
>   *all honor and glory is yours, almighty Father (God),*
> *now and for ever.* **Amen.**

The bread is broken and the bread and cup shared with all who will serve. While the bread and cup are given to the congregation, the congregation may sing hymns, or there may be vocal or instrumental music. It is particularly effective if the people can sing hymns and songs from memory during communion. When all have received, the Lord's Table is put in order.

A prayer after Holy Communion:

> *Almighty God,*
>   *we thank you that in your great love*
>   *you have fed us with the spiritual food and drink*
>   *of the Body and Blood of your Son Jesus Christ,*
>   *and have given us a foretaste*
>   *of your heavenly banquet.*
> *Grant that this Sacrament*
>   *may be to us a comfort in affliction,*
>   *and a pledge of our inheritance in that kingdom*
>   *where there is no death, neither sorrow nor crying,*
>   *but the fullness of joy with all your saints;*
>   *through Jesus Christ our Savior. Amen. (Anglican)*

✚ *Prayer of Thanksgiving When Holy Communion Is Not Celebrated*

If Holy Communion is celebrated, continue the service using the Prayer of Great Thanksgiving (page 112).

When Holy Communion is not celebrated, the pastor may offer the following final prayer of thanks to God:

God of love, we thank you
*   for all with which you have blessed us*
*   even to this day:*
for the gift of joy in days of health and strength
*   and for the gifts of your abiding presence*
*   and promise in days of pain and grief.*
We praise you for home and friends,
*   and for our baptism and place in your church*
*   with all who have faithfully lived and died.*
Above all else we thank you for Jesus,
*   who knew our griefs,*
*   who died our death and rose for our sake,*
*   and who lives and prays for us.*
And as he taught us, so now we pray: The Lord's
Prayer, see 117. (United Methodist)

O God of grace,
*   you have given us new and living hope*
*   in Jesus Christ.*
We thank you that by dying Christ
*   destroyed the power of death,*
*   and by rising from the grave*
*   opened the way to eternal life.*
Help us to know that because he lives, we shall live also;
*   and that neither death nor life,*
*   nor things present nor things to come*
*   shall be able to separate us from your love*
*   in Christ Jesus our Lord. (Presbyterian)*

✛ *The Lord's Prayer*

Every Christian in every place and every generation has prayed the Lord's Prayer in weekly worship and other gatherings of the people of God. In a small chapel on the slopes of the Mount of Olives, where Jesus prepared for his own death, Jesus' prayer is found in hundreds of different languages, testifying to its universal power. When the disciples asked Jesus how to pray, these words are what he taught. The prayer's final ascription of power and glory eternally seals the whole service with a doxology of faith.

The pastor may lead the whole congregation in praying the Lord's Prayer. While the prayer may also be sung by a soloist or choir, the Lord's Prayer is an ideal way to engage the entire congregation. Choose the text that is most familiar to the gathered congregation, and print it in the bulletin for the sake of guests.

The Lord's Prayer: Ecumenical Text, is a prayer recognized throughout the English-speaking world among all denominations:

> *Our Father in heaven,*
> *hallowed be your name,*
> *your kingdom come,*
> *your will be done, on earth as in heaven.*
> *Give us today our daily bread.*
> *Forgive us our sins*
> *as we forgive those who sin against us.*
> *Save us from the time of trial*
> *and deliver us from evil.*
> *For the kingdom, the power, and the glory are yours*
> *now and for ever. Amen.*

The Lord's Prayer: Traditional Text # 1, comes from the 1549 *English Book of Common Prayer:*

Our Father, who art in heaven,
  hallowed be thy name.
Thy kingdom come,
  thy will be done on earth as it is in heaven.
Give us this day our daily bread.
And forgive us our trespasses,
  as we forgive those who trespass against us.
And lead us not into temptation,
  but deliver us from evil.
For thine is the kingdom, and the power, and the glory,
forever.
  Amen.

The Lord's Prayer: Traditional Text # 2, comes from the King James Version of the prayer from Mathew 6:9-13:

Our Father, who art in heaven,
  hallowed be thy name;
Thy kingdom come,
  thy will be done, on earth as it is in heaven.
Give us this day our daily bread;
  and forgive us our debts,
  as we forgive our debtors;
and lead us not into temptation,
  but deliver us from evil.
For thine is the kingdom and the power and the glory,
forever.
  Amen.

✛ *Commendations and Final Prayers*

The Commendation is the most essential and final response to the proclamation of death and resurrection; the good news of life-everlasting is extended to the deceased! The promise of life without end has now encompassed the one who has died. This offering of the deceased to God parallels Jesus' own commendation at his death: "Father, into thy hands I commend my Spirit" (Luke 23:46 KJV).

Facing the body of the deceased and closing the coffin bring home to the mourners the reality of death and are times when the support of pastor and Christian community is important. The pastor may also wish to stand beside the casket or urn and place hands on it during this prayer.

If the service takes place at the location of burial, the Committal may be substituted for the Commendation.

One or more of the following prayers may be offered, or other prayers may be used. These prayers may take the form of a pastoral prayer, a series of shorter prayers, or a litany. Intercessions, commendations of life, and thanksgivings are also appropriate here.

Commendation of one another to God:

> *God of us all, your love never ends.*
> *When all else fails, you still are God.*
> *We pray to you for one another in our need,*
>   *and for all, anywhere, who mourn with us this day.*
> *To those who doubt, give light;*
>   *to those who are weak, strength;*
>   *to all who have sinned, mercy;*
>   *to all who sorrow, your peace.*
> *Keep true in us*
>   *the love with which we hold one another.*
> *In all our ways we trust you.*
> *And to you,*
>   *with your Church on earth and in heaven,*
>   *we offer honor and glory, now and for ever. Amen.*
> *(United Methodist)*

119

A commendation of the deceased and one another to God:

> *O God, all that you have given us is yours.*
> *As first you gave* Name of the deceased *to us,*
> *now we give* Name of the deceased *back to you.*

> *For our* brother/sister, Name of the deceased,
> *let us pray to our Lord Jesus Christ who said,*
> *"I am Resurrection and I am Life."*
> *Lord, you consoled Martha and Mary in their distress;*
> *draw near to us who mourn for* Name of the deceased,
> *and dry the tears of those who weep.* **Hear us, Lord.**
> *You wept at the grave of Lazarus, your friend;*
> *comfort us in our sorrow.* **Hear us, Lord.**
> *You raised the dead to life;*
> *give to our* brother/sister *eternal life.* **Hear us, Lord.**
> *You promised paradise to the thief who repented;*
> *bring our* brother/sister *to the joys of heaven.*
> **Hear us, Lord.**
> *Our* brother/sister *was washed in Baptism*
> *and anointed with the Holy Spirit;*
> *give* him/her *fellowship with all your saints.*
> **Hear us, Lord.**
> He/she *was nourished with your Body and Blood;*
> *grant* him/her *a place at the table*
> *in your heavenly kingdom.* **Hear us, Lord.**
> *Comfort us in our sorrows*
> *at the death of our* brother/sister;
> *let our faith be our consolation,*
> *and eternal life our hope.*

Silence may be kept.

The pastor concludes with the following prayer:

> *Lord Jesus Christ, we commend to you*
> *our* brother/sister,

120

Name of the deceased, *who was reborn by water*
and the Spirit in Holy Baptism.
Grant that his/her *death*
  may recall to us your victory over death,
  and be an occasion for us
  to renew our trust in your Father's love.
Give us, we pray,
  the faith to follow where you have led the way;
  and where you live and reign
  with the Father and the Holy Spirit,
  to the ages of ages. Amen. (Anglican)

The pastor, with others if desired, standing near the coffin or urn, may lay hands on it, continuing:

Receive Name of the deceased
  into the arms of your mercy.
Raise Name of the deceased *up with all your people.*
Receive us also, and raise us into a new life.
Help us so to love and serve you in this world
  that we may enter into your joy in the world to come.
  Amen. (United Methodist)

Commendation of the deceased alone:

Into your hands, O merciful Savior,
  we commend your servant Name of the deceased.
Acknowledge, we humbly beseech you,
  a sheep of your own fold,
  a lamb of your own flock,
  a sinner of your own redeeming.
Receive Name of the deceased
  into the arms of your mercy,
  into the blessed rest of everlasting peace,
  and into the glorious company of the saints of light.
Amen. (United Methodist & Anglican & Lutheran)

121

An ancient commendation from the Western Rite (Roman Catholic):

> *Make speed to aid* Name of the deceased,
>   *ye saints of God;*
> *Come for to meet* him/her,
>   *ye angels of the Lord;*
> *Receiving* his/her *soul,*
>   *presenting* him/her *before the face of the most highest.*
> *May Christ receive thee, who has called thee;*
>   *and may angels bear you into the bosom of Abraham.*
> *Receiving* his/her *soul;*
>   *presenting* him/her
>   *before the face of the most highest.*
> *Rest eternal grant unto* him/her, *O Lord,*
>   *and let light perpetual shine upon* him/her.

A commendation from *The Book of Common Prayer*:

> *Give rest, O Christ, to your servants with your saints,*
>   *where sorrow and pain are no more,*
>   *neither sighing, but life everlasting.*
> *You only are immortal,*
>   *the creator and maker of all people;*
>   *and we are mortal, formed of the earth,*
>   *and to earth shall we return.*
> *For so did you ordain when you created us, saying,*
>   *"You are dust, and to dust you shall return."*
> *All of us go down to the dust;*
>   *yet even at the grave we make our song:*
>   *Alleluia, alleluia, alleluia.*
> *Give rest, O Christ, to your servant(s) with your saints,*
>   *where sorrow and pain are no more,*
>   *neither sighing, but life everlasting. (Anglican)*

✠ *Dismissals with Blessings*

The service of worship now closes. These final prayers encourage the congregation to uphold and care for one another in grief and hope.

The pastor, facing the people, may offer one or more of the following prayers of sending forth or other Dismissal with Blessing. To honor the deceased and the family, the congregation stands for the dismissal and remains standing until the family leaves the worship space.

Now may the God of peace
who brought back from the dead our Lord Jesus,
   the great Shepherd of the sheep,
   by the blood of the eternal covenant,
make you complete in everything good
   so that you may do God's will,
working among us that which is pleasing in God's sight,
   through Jesus Christ;
to whom be the glory for ever and ever. Amen.
(United Methodist, Hebrews 13:20-21, alt.)

The peace of God which passes all understanding
   keep your hearts and minds
   in the knowledge and love of God,
   and of his Son Jesus Christ our Lord.
And the blessing of God Almighty,
   the Father, Son, and Holy Spirit,
be among you and remain with you always. Amen.
(United Methodist)

Now may the Father
   from whom every family
   in heaven and on earth is named,
   according to the riches of God's glory,
grant you to be strengthened with might
   through God's Spirit in your inner being,
   that Christ may dwell in your hearts through faith;

that you, being rooted and grounded in love,
may be able to comprehend with all the saints
what is the breadth and length and height and depth,
and to know the love of Christ
which surpasses knowledge,
that you may be filled with all the fullness of God.
Amen.
(United Methodist, paraphrase of Ephesians 3:14-19)

Now to the One who by the power at work within us
who is able to do far more abundantly
than all that we ask or think,
to God be glory in the church
and in Christ Jesus
to all generations, for ever and ever. Amen.
(United Methodist, Ephesians 3:20-21, alt.)

Glory to the Father,
who has woven garments of glory for the resurrection;
Worship to the Son,
who was clothed in them at his rising;
Thanksgiving to the Spirit,
who keeps them for all the saints;
One nature in three, to God be praise.
(Syrian Orthodox)

The pastor now leads the recession from the place of worship. The pastor leads the casket or urn from the sanctuary to the hearse or funeral car or to the gravesite.

Church bells may be rung as the casket and family leave the church.

The Committal follows at the final resting place.

CHAPTER SIX

GRAVESIDE COMMITTALS

The Committal is a brief service immediately prior to burial, often at a gravesite, columbarium, or mausoleum. This committal may happen either before a memorial service or after a funeral, as an extension of the commendation at the end of the full service.

The final disposition of the body has many possibilities. Burial of the body or ashes in the earth or a mausoleum, scattering of ashes on the earth or into the sea, or placement in a columbarium are all common. The body may also be donated for medical purposes. Or the family may wish to take the ashes home and preserve them there.

"Green Funerals" are a newer tradition where bodies are not embalmed, the caskets are of biodegradable materials, and the burials are in places where the bodies are more quickly returned to the earth.

If the only service is a graveside service, the pastor should preface this Committal with prayers and Scriptures from the full Service of Death and Resurrection. Typically, the service is shorter, with a brief homily and limited witnessing.

Watch the weather. Cold air, heavy winds, snow, or rain may dictate a very short service. Be alert to all possibilities.

The people gather informally. The pastor may lead a procession of the casket from the funeral vehicle to the grave, or simply stand next to the casket that has already been placed above the grave. The pastor stands at the end of the casket closest to the head of the deceased.

Typically, everyone stands, with the exception of the family as seats are available.

If the family requests that there be military, fraternal, or other rites in addition to the Christian Committal, the pastor should approve such rites and plan carefully the sequence and interrelationship of these services so that the service is not interrupted. Some pastors allow such rituals and honors only before a service begins or immediately before the Committal. This pattern preserves the integrity of the Christian service and allows the last words to be a word of God's grace. Yet, certain acts, especially the giving of a national flag, rifle volleys, and the music "Taps" may best follow the Committal. See page 11 for more details.

Prayers and lessons appropriate for a service for a child or youth, or for other distinctive occasions, as found in the resources for Services of Death and Resurrection (page 40) may be used instead of the following.

✚ *The Consecration of a Grave*

If the grave is in a place that has not previously been set apart for Christian burial, the pastor may offer the following prayer, either before the service of Committal or at some other time.

O God, whose blessed Son
  was laid in a sepulcher in the garden:
Bless, we pray, this grave,
  and grant that he/she *whose body* is/is to be *buried*
  here may dwell with Christ in paradise,
and may come to your heavenly kingdom;
  through your Son Jesus Christ our Lord. Amen.
(Anglican)

✛ *Greetings*

When the people have gathered, the pastor stands at the head of the casket or next to the urn and offers one or more of the following:

In the midst of life, we are in death;
from whom can we seek help?
Our help is in the name of the Lord
who made heaven and earth.
God who raised Christ from the dead
will give life to your mortal bodies also
through the Spirit that dwells in you.
(United Methodist)

Everyone the Father gives to me will come to me;
I will never turn away anyone who believes in me.
God who raised Jesus Christ from the dead
will also give new life to our mortal bodies
through God's indwelling Spirit.
My heart, therefore, is glad, and my spirit rejoices;
my body also shall rest in hope.
You will show me the path of life;
in your presence there is fullness of joy,
and in your right hand are pleasures for evermore.
(Anglican, alt.)

Job declared:
I know that my Redeemer lives,
and that at the last God will stand upon the earth.
(Job 19:25)

The steadfast love of the Lord never ceases,
God's mercies never come to an end;
they are new every morning,
so great is God's faithfulness. (Lamentation 3:22-23)

We know that if the earthly tent we live in is destroyed,

we have a building from God,
a house not made with hands, eternal in the heavens.
(2 Corinthians 5:1)

Listen, I will tell you a mystery!
We will not all die, but we will all be changed.
For this perishable body must put on imperishability,
and this mortal body must put on immortality.
Then the saying that is written will be fulfilled:
"Death has been swallowed up in victory."
"Where, O death, is your victory?
Where, O death, is your sting?"
But thanks be to God,
who gives us the victory
through our Lord Jesus Christ.
(1 Corinthians 15:51-57, excerpts)

Therefore my heart is glad, and my soul rejoices;
my body also dwells secure.
Lord, show me the path of life;
in your presence there is fullness of joy,
in your right hand are pleasures forevermore.
(Psalm 16:9, 11, alt.)

Blessed are those who mourn,
for they will be comforted. (Matthew 5:4)

✛ *Opening Prayers*

The pastor offers one of the following prayers or an extemporaneous prayer:

O God, you have ordered this wonderful world
and know all things in earth and in heaven.
Give us such faith that by day and by night,
at all times and in all places,
we may without fear commit ourselves
and those dear to us
to your never-failing love,
in this life and in the life to come. Amen.
(United Methodist)

Eternal Father, God of all consolation,
be our refuge and strength in sorrow.
As your Son, our Lord Jesus Christ,
by dying for us conquered death,
and by rising again restored us to life,
enable us to go forward in faith to meet Christ,
that, when our life on earth has ended,
we may be united with all who love Christ
in your heavenly kingdom,
where every tear will be wiped away;
through Jesus Christ our Lord. Amen.
(Australian, alt.)

☩ *Scriptures*

One of the following or other Scriptures may be read:

Blessed be the God and Father of our Lord Jesus Christ!
By God's great mercy
we have been born anew to a living hope
  through the resurrection of Jesus Christ
  from the dead,
and to an inheritance
  that is imperishable, undefiled, and unfading,
  kept in heaven for you.
In this you rejoice, though now for a little while
you suffer trials
  so that the genuineness of your faith
  may prove itself worthy
  at the revelation of Jesus Christ.
Without having seen Jesus Christ, yet you love him;
though you do not now see him,
  you believe in Christ and rejoice
  with unutterable and exalted joy.
As the harvest of your faith
you reap the salvation of your souls.
(United Methodist, adapted from 1 Peter 1:3-9)

Jesus said: "Very truly, I tell you,
  unless a grain of wheat falls into the earth and dies,
  it remains just a single grain;
  but if the single grain dies, it bears much fruit.
Those who love their life lose it,
  and those who hate their life in this world
  will keep it for eternal life.
Whoever serves me must follow me,
  and where I am, there will my servant be also.
Whoever serves me, the Father will honor."
(John 12:24-26, alt.)

✛ *Committals*

Standing at the head of the coffin, facing it, and laying hands on the coffin or urn, the pastor says:

> *Almighty God,*
> > *into your hands we commend your* son/daughter,
> Name of the deceased,
> > *in sure and certain hope of resurrection to eternal life*
> > *through Jesus Christ our Lord. Amen.*
> *This body we commit to the ground*
> > *(to the elements, to its resting place),*
> > *earth to earth, ashes to ashes, dust to dust.*
> *Blessed are the dead who die in the Lord.*
> *Yes, says the Spirit, they will rest from their labors*
> > *for their deeds follow them.*
> *(United Methodist & Anglican)*

For a burial at sea:

> *In sure and certain hope of the resurrection*
> *to eternal life,*
> > *through our Lord Jesus Christ,*
> > *the spring of life-giving water,*
> *we commend to almighty God* Name of the deceased
> > *and we commit this body to the deep. (Andy Langford)*

The pastor may pour or sprinkle a small amount of earth upon the casket. Some pastors bring a small container with dry earth for this sign-act. Or, the pastor may cast earth upon the casket as it is lowered into the grave. Other members of the funeral party may also participate in these actions. In some areas, persons toss flowers into the grave or leave them upon the casket. These actions may also occur at the end of the Committal.

✛ *Closing Prayers*

One or more of the following or other prayers is offered:

Gracious God,
we thank you for those we love but see no more.
Receive into your arms
your servant Name of the deceased,
    and grant that increasing in knowledge
    and love of you,
    he/she *may go from strength to strength*
    in service to your heavenly kingdom;
through Jesus Christ our Lord. Amen.
(United Methodist)

Almighty God,
    look with pity upon the sorrow of your servants,
    for whom we pray.
Amidst things they cannot understand,
    help them to trust in your care.
Bless them and keep them.
Make your face to shine upon them,
    and give them peace. Amen. (United Methodist)

O God, whose days are without end,
    make us deeply aware of the shortness
    and uncertainty of our human life.
Raise us from sin into love and goodness,
    that when we depart this life we may rest in Christ
    and receive the blessing Christ has promised
    to those who love and serve him:
"Come, you blessed of my Father,
    receive the kingdom prepared for you
    from the foundation of the world."
Grant this, merciful Father,
    through Jesus Christ our Mediator and Redeemer.
    Amen. (Book of Services)

O Lord, support us all the day long of our troubled life,
until the shadows lengthen and the evening comes,
and the busy world is hushed,
and the fever of life is over and our work is done.
Then in your mercy grant us a safe lodging,
and a holy rest, and peace at the last;
through Jesus Christ our Lord. Amen.
(attributed to John Henry Newman, adapted by United Methodist & Lutheran & Presbyterian)

God of boundless compassion,
our only sure comfort in distress:
Look tenderly upon your children
overwhelmed by loss and sorrow.
Lighten our darkness with your presence
and assure us of your love.
Enable us to see beyond this place and time
to your eternal kingdom,
promised to all who love you in Christ the Lord. Amen.
(Presbyterian)

Eternal God, you have shared with us
the life of Name of the deceased.
Before he/she *was ours,* he/she *is yours.*
For all that Name of the deceased
has given us to make us what we are,
for that of him/her *which lives and grows in each of us,*
and for his/her *life that in your love will never end,*
we give you thanks.
As now we offer Name of the deceased
back into your arms,
comfort us in our loneliness,
strengthen us in our weakness,
and give us courage to face the future unafraid.
Draw those of us who remain in this life
closer to one another,

the names of particular persons may be spoken aloud
make us faithful to serve one another,
and give us to know that peace and joy
which is eternal life;
through Jesus Christ our Lord. Amen. (United Methodist)

Merciful God,
  you heal the broken in heart
  and bind up the wounds of the afflicted.
Strengthen us in our weakness,
  calm our troubled spirits,
  and dispel our doubts and fears.
In Christ's rising from the dead,
  you conquered death and opened the gates
  to everlasting life.
Renew our trust in you
  that by the power of your love
  we shall one day be brought together again
  with our sister/brother Name of the deceased.
Grant this, we pray, through Jesus Christ our Lord.
Amen. (Lutheran)

Prayer for a stillborn child:

All-loving and caring God, Parent of us all,
  you know our grief in our loss,
  for you too suffered the death of your child.
Give us strength to go forward from this day,
  trusting, where we do not understand,
  that your love never ends.
When all else fails, you still are God.

We thank you for the life and hope
  that you give through the resurrection
  of your Son Jesus Christ.
We pray to you for one another in our need,

and for all, anywhere, who mourn with us this day.
To those who doubt, give light;
*   to those who are weak, strength;*
*   to all who have sinned, mercy;*
*   to all who sorrow, your peace. Amen.*
(United Methodist)

The Lord's Prayer may follow: see page 117. A hymn or song may be sung.

✛ *Dismissals with Blessings*

The pastor dismisses the people with the following or another blessing of God upon the people:

Now to the One who is able to keep you from falling,
and to make you stand without blemish
in the presence of God's glory with rejoicing,
to the only God our Savior, through Jesus Christ our Lord,
be glory, majesty, power, and authority,
before all time and now and forever. Amen.
(United Methodist, from Jude 24-25 [KJV], alt.)

Go in peace,
and may the God of peace,
who brought back from the dead our Lord Jesus,
make you complete in everything good
so that you may do God's will,
working among us that which is pleasing
in God's sight,
through Jesus Christ,
to whom be the glory forever and ever! Amen.
(Hebrews 13:20-12)

After the dismissal with blessing, the pastor signals the going forth. The pastor may approach and greet the grieving family and other participants and grant them a final blessing and farewell. Persons may also remain to greet one another with signs of support and love.

CHAPTER SEVEN

MINISTRY WITH THE GRIEVING

Grief at a loss due to death neither begins nor ends with the pastoral offices included in this resource. Ebenezer Scrooge, in Charles Dickens' *A Christmas Carol in Prose,* watched with the Ghost of Christmas Future paid professional mourners at his own funeral. Paid mourners were a common part of Victorian English funerals.

Today, each individual bears grief. The wise use of the resources in this book give clarity to the role of faith and the presence of God, but they do not resolve all the issues of grief. Many people are aware of the stages of grief—anger, grief, denial, bargaining, guilt, panic, depression, illness, and others—and many of these reactions invite pastoral support.

It is essential that ongoing congregational life in its totality be centered in the Christian gospel, which is a message of death and resurrection. The way in which persons deal with all death—past, present, and future—will depend upon how central this good news has become in their lives.

Reentry into the community by the chief mourners following the service takes time and can be facilitated by the supportive ministry of the church. If the funeral or memorial service itself did not include Holy Communion, the pastor may take the Eucharist to the family, perhaps at the first visit following the service.

Continuing support of representatives of the community, including ministries of prayer and worship as appropriate, is essential in the long-term process by which those who mourn find healing. In addition, many resources have been created and written to assist in grief at death. These resources include significant books, programs of scheduled brochures mailed to a family, and others.

Recurring memorial acts and services are occasions both of healing and of celebration. Mourners are especially open to supportive ministries on such occasions as Christmas, holidays, birthdays, and anniversaries of marriage or of death. Celebration of All Saints Day or Sunday and other annual memorial services can also be particularly helpful.

At any given time, in any congregation, there are people at many different points of grief. Some persons have just been diagnosed with a life-threatening illness. Other people care for family and friends who are dying. Some folk are in the last stages of life, while others mourn the recent loss of a parent, child, family member, or friend. Good pastoral care addresses all of these persons, not just in pastoral counseling but in the liturgies of the church. Preach regularly on dying and death. Address the realities of grief. Give opportunities to name the deceased and those who are bereaved. For example, in some Jewish communities, the dead are lifted by name in the sabbath worship for a full year after death.

✛ *Prayers*

The following is a prayer for Memorial Day, the first Monday in May in the United States, which honors the nation's war dead:

Almighty God,
before whom stand the living and the dead,
we your children,
whose mortal life is but a hand's breadth,
give thanks to you:
For all those through whom
you have blessed our pilgrimage,
whose lives that have empowered us,
whose influence is a healing grace...
We lift up thankful hearts.

For the dear friends and family members
whose faces we see no more,
but whose love is with us for ever...
We lift up thankful hearts.

For the teachers and companions
of our childhood and youth,
and for the members of our household of faith
who worship you now in heaven...
We lift up thankful hearts.

For those who sacrificed themselves,
our brothers and sisters who have given their lives
for the sake of others...
We lift up thankful hearts.

That we may hold them all in continual remembrance,
and ever think of them as with you
in that city whose gates are not shut by day
and where there is no night...
We lift up thankful hearts.

That we may now be dedicated to working for a world
*   where labor is rewarded,*
*   fear dispelled, and the nations made one,*
*   O Lord, save your people and bless your heritage.*
Day by day we magnify you,
*   and worship your name, for ever and ever. Amen.*
(John Hunter)

On the anniversary of a death, the pastor may offer this prayer, which comes out of the Jewish tradition and is adapted for use in Christian congregations. It may also be used on All Saints Day or Sunday, a Homecoming, or cemetery Decoration Day, or Memorial Day, or any other occasion when the dead are remembered:

Everliving God,
*   this day revives in us memories of loved ones*
*   who are no more.*
What happiness we shared when they walked among us.
What joy, when, loving and being loved,
*   we lived our lives together.*
Their memory is a blessing for ever.
Months or years may have passed,
*   and still we feel near to them.*
Our hearts yearn for them.
Though the bitter grief has softened,
*   a duller pain abides;*
*   for the place where once they stood is empty now.*
The links of life are broken,
*   but the links of love and longing cannot break.*
Their souls are bound up in ours for ever.
We see them now with the eye of memory,
*   their faults forgiven, their virtues grown larger.*
So does goodness live, and weakness fade from sight.
We remember them with gratitude
*   and bless their names.*
Their memory is a blessing for ever.

And we remember as well the members
   who but yesterday were part
   of our congregation and community.
To all who cared for us and labored for all people,
   we pay tribute.
May we prove worthy
   of carrying on the tradition of our faith,
   for now the task is ours.
Their souls are bound up in ours for ever.
We give you thanks
   that they now live and reign with you.
As a great cloud of witnesses,
   they surround us with their blessings,
   and offer you hymns of praise and thanksgiving.
They are alive for ever more. Amen. (United Methodist,
Andy Langford, based on Jewish Memorial Prayer, alt.)

O God, today brings us sad memories.
Sometimes we can forget,
   yet deep down the pain remains,
   for you have given us tender hearts.
Even a glimpse of a place or a photograph,
   the sound of a tune or a word,
   and especially a day like this can make us feel again
   that emptiness which nothing on earth can fill.
May we not be overcome by our sorrow
   as those who have no hope.
Help us face life with steadfast faith,
   remembering that the one we loved
   has been added to that unseen cloud of witnesses
   who constantly surround us.
Hasten the time when the memories which distress us
   will be the very things
   that enrich our life and deepen our love;
through Jesus Christ our Lord. Amen. (Australian)

ACKNOWLEDGMENTS

Scripture, unless otherwise indicated, is adapted from the New Revised Standard Version of the Bible, ©1989 by Division of Christian Education of the National Council of the Churches of Christ in the United States of America and is used by permission.

"United Methodist" resources come from *The United Methodist Book of Worship,* © 1992 The United Methodist Publishing House. See the Acknowledgements of that resource for a comprehensive history of the copyright of these resources.

"The Book of Services" refers to an early draft of official United Methodist liturgies, included in *The Book of Services* © 1985 The United Methodist Publishing House.

"Anglican" refers to the Liturgy of the Episcopal Church of North America, whose precedents have been the basis of many of the prayer books in the English-speaking world. Although copyright permission is not required for use of items from *The Book of Common Prayer* (Episcopal 1979), as a courtesy, we acknowledge indebtedness to this source.

"Lutheran" refers to prayers from *Evangelical Lutheran Worship* © 2006 Evangelical Lutheran Church in America, published by Augsburg Fortress, Publishers.

"Presbyterian" refers to prayers from *Book of Common Worship* © 1993 Westminster/John Knox Press, Louisville: Kentucky. These prayers are from The Presbyterian Church (U.S.A.) and Cumberland Presbyterian Church.

"Australian" refers to *Uniting in Worship* © 1988 The Uniting Church in Australia Assembly Commission on Liturgy. This is the dominant Protestant church in Australia.

Printed in the USA
CPSIA information can be obtained
at www.ICGtesting.com
LVHW011214080823
754629LV00004B/312